OUR CAMINO DIARY

2 PEOPLE, 540 MILES, AND ONE 1 AMAZING JOURNEY.

BRETT JACKSON
KAREN BEECHAM

BRETTISH BOOKS

Dedication

*This book is dedicated to all who are on a pilgrimage.
May you achieve your goal, and enjoy the journey.*

Ultreia et Suseia (Onwards and Upwards)

→

Special Thanks

*To all the pilgrims we met, and spent time with. You helped make
this the most amazing journey ever.*

*Also, to our friends, and family, for all your support along the
way, and especially to you the reader, for buying this special book
and sharing our journey.*

INTRODUCTION TO OUR CAMINO DIARY

Hello and welcome to *Our Camino Diary*.

This book is a combination of our handwritten journals, a blog (now defunct), a few photographs of over 10 thousand which were taken, and comments about our experiences; mental, physical and spiritual, as we walked along *The Way*.

Thankyou for buying this book, and giving us the chance to share our journey.

Buen Camino (Good Walk / Good Life).
Brett and Karen

This pencil drawing of the front cover of this book was sketched by Kath Graham - A pilgrim from New Zealand who we met on "The Way".

The chances are, that if you are reading this book, you probably already know what the Camino is... however, if you are new to this, then let me break it down for you.

The Camino / El Camino / The Way / The Way of St. James is a pilgrimage to visit the resting place of St. James in Santiago in Spain. Some pilgrims even walk the extra 3 days to Finisterre (literally translated as "the end of the world"). There are many Camino routes, including the Camino Norte, Camino Portuguese, Camino Frances, and more. The words "El Camino" literally mean "The Way".

For centuries, people have walked "The Way of St. James" (Camino Frances). This pilgrimage takes you on a journey by foot or cycle starting in St.Jean Pied de Port in France, traversing over 540 miles, (800+km) through the Pyrenees mountains, across the Navarre, Rioja. Castilla y Leon, and

Galicia regions, across the Meseta, passing famous landmarks, such as Alto De Perdon with its sheet metal cutouts of Pilgrims throughout the ages, cities such as Pamplona, Leon, Burgos, and Santiago, sights such as the Cruz de Ferro (Iron Cross which pilgrims place a stone at the foot of to say goodbye to a loved one, or let go of a particular trouble in their life), across rivers, mountains, woodlands, vine groves, and into the beautiful city of Santiago de Compostela, where you can visit the Cathedral with many other pilgrims.

On the 29th April 2019, my wife (Karen) and I made our trek to St.Jean-Pied-de-Port, and the start of our adventure. We invited friends and family to follow us as we journeyed from St.Jean Pied de Port in France, through the Pyrenees mountains into Spain, through the Navarre and Rioja regions, across the Meseta, and further on to Santiago de Compostela, as we trekked to the tomb and resting place of St. James, laid to rest in the Cathedral of Santiago de Compostela.

An Important thing to note here, is that the Camino is a major part of Spanish life, and because of this, it is mandatory for Spanish students to complete the last 100km of the Camino, as a part of their life skills, and something to put onto their Curriculum Vitae.

→

As you journey along the Camino, you can't help but notice scallop shells everywhere. They can be as small as your fingernail, or as large as a wall. Most Pilgrims will wear one on their backpack. A lot of arrows look like shells.

If you look at the shell, you will see it fans out, and has ridges going from the outside of the fan, in to a central spot.

In the same way, the Camino does exactly that. The scallop shell is an important symbol on the Camino, pointing from all parts of the world to Santiago, because each walker comes from different parts of the world, but all end up in the same place.

You will also notice arrows, they come in different shapes and sizes, on the sides of buildings, on roads, and sometimes in the most unusual of places. They are mostly yellow, but can also come in different colours, materials and shapes.

I based this sketch on the map you will probably find in your Pilgrims passport, except I have changed the locations for the places we stayed along the way. Each place named on this map has a journal entry in 'Our Camino Diary'. This journey took us 40 days from start to end and included several rest days.

WHY ARE WE DOING THE CAMINO?

Bretts Journey

In March 2012, I took a phone call, and received some sad news that my father had passed away in Valencia, in Spain. My health took a nosedive and I was unable to attend his funeral in the county of Devon, as I could not make the lengthy journey from Lincolnshire in the UK.

Still grieving, I walked the Camino 7 years later, taking a stone from my back garden, and left it at the foot of the Cruz de Ferro with my fathers name on it, and a small sentiment.

I said a prayer, and left my stone at the foot of the Cross, as my way to say goodbye to him, and bring closure. I know my father is no longer here, but in my heart, he will never die, and I will always remember him.

This part added on 30th September 2021:

Looking back now, this act of letting go, really helped with my healing process, and life is able to carry on, now that I know I had the chance to say goodbye.

Karens Journey

As a Methodist Minister we are given a precious gift of a

Sabbatical every 7 years. I was introduced to the Camino by another Minister, and instantly felt that I would like to do this walk as part of my Sabbatical. All of our children had either left home, or were old enough to stay on their own.

I was moving appointments, so it felt like the right time to take some time out to evaluate what had gone well, what to leave behind, and what new things I would like to do. This time away was invaluable to me. It has changed my ministry, the way we are, our understanding of each other, and the importance of listening to other peoples stories.

PREPARATION

How we prepared for the Camino.
In the months coming up to our adventure, Karen and I would spend hours watching videos on YouTube, created by people who had completed the Camino. We read books and journals (much like this one) and took away the most important pieces.

The videos we watched included:
- The *Count Everything* guy, with his useful videos about language, feet issues, Camino Cat and much more.
- Efren Gonzales from his 2017 series of videos, as he visits each place along the way.
- *The Way* with Martin Sheen and Emilio Estevez which we watched on TV and Netflix.
- *The Way* documentary with celebrities, which we also watched on television.

These videos would help us with such things as:
Items to include in your backpack, best ways to avoid blisters, taking two ATM cards with you, and much more.

→

How much does the Camino cost?
In a nutshell? We spent 200 euros per week.

After watching the videos, we learnt that the general costs are for the following items.

Albergues cost between 6 and 15 euros per night.

Food costs between 6 and 10 euros per meal

Washing costs between 2 and 6 euros (although, hand washing is free)

Supermarket shopping usually costs around 25 euros per week.

Extras? Think carefully before you cost up extras, because… if you buy it, you carry it, and believe me, every single gram matters. I ended up taking a solar panel, which I used every day to charge the USB battery pack for my phone, and a life straw water filtration device, which never even came out of its packet. Although the solar panel was useful, all the time, and it was a great conversation-starter, it was also extra weight in my pack.

If you can, take two ATM cards with you. In case you lose one.

Packing for the Camino
Each Pilgrim takes a backpack of items with them, and these vary.

Karen's backpack and mine were slightly different, and I have included what we packed with us in the next section. This isn't an official guide on what to pack, but we did our research and looked through guidebooks and videos to ensure we were packing the right equipment.

As part of our trip to the camping store, we bought some Quechua, 40 litre backpacks, and some waterproof bags. We labeled these bags, which allowed us to separate our sleeping bags, washing stuff, clothes and electrical items, and meant that if it did rain along the way, our packs might get wet, but the stuff inside them wouldn't.

I have split up the next section of this diary into his and hers section. Although this is not an official guide to the Camino, it helps to see what we took with us.

We both took:

- Quechua 40L backpack from Decathlon
- Decathlon Waterproof roll down bags with clips. (We labelled each of our bags with permanent markers).
- Karrimor walking boots (labelled at the back of the boot, for easy identification in the various shoe storage places at each Albergue (Hostel)).
- Silk lined socks with Merino Wool outers (aka Antib-lister socks). The silk wicks the moisture away from the skin keeping it dry and blister free, while the merino wool keeps your feet warm. The silk liner also clings to your feet and the wool outer rubs against the silk liner, instead of rubbing against your feet. Because the silk is almost friction free, this literally eliminates blisters as long as you keep them dry. (Don't forget to wash them every day, and on hot days, you may need to stop walking to dry you feet, eat, rest and maybe swap socks too.

We labeled each waterproof bag and organised them into different sizes. This made things easier, and kept our kit dry, in case of showers.

→

Bretts stuff

BJ1 - Electrical Stuff / Gadgets.

Kindle x 1

Fold-up Keyboard x 1

Easy Acc Power pack (portable battery for charging mobile phone).

Solar Panel x 1

USB Mini Lead x 1

USB Lightening Lead x 1

240v USB Plug x 1

240v UK to EU x 1

iPod x 1

Earbuds (for listening to music) x 1

BJ2 - Misc

Emergency Water Bottle x 1

Water Filter x 1

First Aid Kit x 1

Knife, Fork, Spoon x 1

Paracord Washing Line x 1 &

- Safety pins x 1 large (for hanging our washing)

- Safety pins x 12 small

Sweets x 3

Spanish Phrasebook x 1

Lush Tin x 1

Lush Shampoo bar x 1

Journal x 1

Pen x 1

Copy of Marriage Documents x 1

Copy of Religious Letter x 1

Itinerary x 1

Bulldog clips x 2

Sticky Notes x 1

BJ3 - Clothes

Tissue x 3

Ziplock Bag x 1

Lightweight Easy-Dry Long-Sleeved Shirt x 1 (bought from Decathlon).

Lightweight Easy-Dry Long-Sleeved Shirt x 1 (wearing)

Lightweight Easy-Dry Zipped Trousers x 1 (These Zip at the knee to turn them into shorts).

Lightweight Easy-Dry Zipped Trousers x 1 (Wearing)

Lightweight Easy-Dry T-shirt x 1

Lightweight Easy-Dry T-shirt x 1 (Wearing).

Anti-Blister Socks x 2 (Double Layered - Merino Wool outers and Silk Inners).

Anti-Blister Socks (Wearing).

Underwear x 2

Underwear (Wearing).

White Short-Sleeved Shirt x 1

Flannel x 1

See-through wash bag (for customs)

BJ4 - Bedding

Sleeping Bag

Slapping Bag Cover

Pillowcase

Glasses Cloth

Earplugs

Spare Shoelaces

Inside my backpack.

Rucksack waterproof cover x 1

Beany with built-in rechargeable USB head torch.

PackaMac x 1

Zip Docs and Wallet

- Passport
- Driving License

10kg Rucksack.

Fingerless Gloves.

Compact Backpack (10kg backpack. For putting valuable into when you leave main pack at Dorm).

Hanging from Rucksack.

Crocks - Rubber shoes.

Carabina

Buff

Vital ID.

Miscellaneous

Camel pack x 1 (I only used this once, when I really needed it).

Carabinas x 2

Carabina and emergency whistle x 1

Elasticated Velcro x 1

Stone (For laying at the foot of the Cruz De Ferro).

Karrimor Hiking boots x 1 pair (Label the back of these with a sharpie, so you can identify your boots).

Elasticized Laces.

Massage ball x 1

ABC Watch x 1

Hat (Bought through the internet from Australia - 100% waterproof and sunproof to prevent skin cancer)

iPhone 6 (all loaded up with Netflix films, and space to take over 10 thousand photos).

Selfie Stick (great for taking photos, but also for watching Netflix in the bunk).

Front Pocket of Backpack

Tissues
Mints
Vaseline stick to prevent chapped lips.
Passport

Wallet
200 Euros
Bank Card x 2 (Just in case you lose one).

Bumbag / Fanny Pack
(For UK Passport and Camino Passport).

Karens Stuff
Drybag 1
Sleeping Bag x 1
Pillowcase x 1
Earplugs x 3
Eye mask x 1

Drybag 2: Orange
Journal x 1
Phone Charger lead (apple) x 1
USB Battery pack with built-in solar panel x 1
Kindle Charger lead x 1
EU Plug x 1
Kindle x 1
Pen x 1
Purse
Reading Glasses x 1
Bank Card and Credit Card

Drybag 3 - Clothing
Sunhat

Towel
Toiletries
Socks x 3
Trousers x 2
Shorts x 1
Strap top x 1
Short sleeve x 2
Long sleeve top x 2
Underwear x 3
Sports bra x 2
Fleece x 1
Hair stuff
Tissues

Miscellaneous

Guidebook (pack pocket)
Sunglasses (Pack Pocket)
Sunscreen (little pouch).
Water Bottle
Waterproofs (top pocket).
Pocket Knife
Sandals (Front)
Compact Backpack.
Safety Pins (Inside Pocket).
Backpack cover (top pocket).
Gloves
Hot Mug
Sweets
Whistle
Tissues
Lip Balm.

Inside the Bumbag,

Lip Balm
Stone (for leaving at Cruz De Ferro).
Buff
Purse
Passport
MP3 player and Headphones.
Cardholder.

→

Camino Spanish

Some common Camino phrases.

Although most countries in the world speak English, you will benefit from learning a little rudimentary Spanish, so that you can get a meal, a bed, or perhaps just a smile because you made the effort.

Even if you have never spoken Spanish before, this small guide should help you on the Camino.

Please note: I am not a qualified Spanish teacher, so some spellings may be wrong, but I have tried to correct them to the best of my ability. This is not intended to be a learning guide, I am simply passing on some of the Spanish we learnt, to help you along your pilgrimage.

The top phrases on the Camino are:

Buen Camino - Good Walk (General greeting, you will probably say this phrase hundreds of times a day, it's like saying hello).

Agua potable - Drinking Water

Agua no potable - Not drinking water

Gracias - Thankyou

Buen Dia - Good Day

Ultreia (not Spanish, but Latin, it means "Onwards", and

you would reply with "et Suseia" which means "and upwards").

Hello - Hola

How to use this guide

The phrases and words in this guide are written in such a way that you can find the English word you are looking for, then you will see the way it is spelt in Spanish, and finally a phonetic guide to help you be able to say the words or phrases. To learn how to pronounce these words and phrases correctly, Karen and I spent some time on YouTube and even downloaded the language learning app Duolingo. There are lots of videos which teach you Camino Spanish.

Example:
English - Spanish - Pronunciation
Hello - Hola - oh-la

General Greetings

Hello - Hola - oh-la

Good Day - Buenos dias - Bwen-os dee-ahs

Hello, good morning - Hola, Beunos Dias - oh-la bwen-os dee-ahs .

Good Day - Buen Dia - Bwen Dee-ah

Good Afternoon - Buenas Tardes - Bwen-ahs Tar-des

Good Night - Buenos Noches - Bwen-os Notches

Goodbye - Ciao - Chow (like now)

Goodbye - Adios - add-ee-oss

See you later - Hasta Luego - aster lou-ay-go

What is your name? - Como se llama? - Commo say yarma

My name is (your name here) - Me llamo (your name here) - may armo (your name here).

How are you? - Que tal - kay tal (like pal)

Good - Beuno - bway-no
Very good - muy bien - mwee bee-en

Top 10 Camino Phrases (with yes or no answers).
Good Way / Have a good walk - Buen Camino - Bwen Cam-ee-no
Hello, Good Morning - Hola, Buenos Dias
Have a good day - Que tenga buen dia.
Put me this - Punga May eso por favor -

Being polite (try not to use muchos gracias too much, this may seem rude, but the Spanish people just speak this way).
Thankyou - Gracias - grath-ee-ahs
Thankyou very much - Muchos Gracias - Moo-chose grass-ee-ahs

Shops
Open - Abierto - ab-ee-heir-toe
Closed - Cerrado - se-rar-doe
Opening Hours - Horarios (de apertura) - orar-ee-ohs de appar-tyou-rah

On the trail,
Drinking Water - Agua potable - agwa pot-a-bull
Not drinking water - Agua no potable - agwa no pot-a-bull

Numbers
Zero - Cero - Say-roe
One - Uno - oo-no
Two - Dos - doss
Three - Tres - trehs
Four - Quatro - kwa-trow (like throw).

Five - Cinqo - sink-oh
Six - Seis - say-es
Seven - Siete - seaa-yet-eh
Eight - Ocho - och-oh
Nine - Neuve - new-eh-veh
Ten - Diez - dee-ezz

People
Sir - Senor - Sen-your
Madam - Senora - Sen-your-ah
Miss - Senorita - Sen-you-rita
Waiter (Man) - Cameraro - Cama-rare-oh
Waiter (Woman) - Camerara - Cama-rare-ah
Albergue Landlord - Hospitalero - Hospital-air-oh

Places
Toilet - Baño - ban-yo
Airport - Aeropuerto - eye-row-pwear-toe
Leon - Leon - Lay-on
Pamplona - Pamp-lone-ah

At a bar / cafe / restaurant
Money - Dinero - din-air-oh
Drinks
Coffee - cafe - kaff-eh
Tea - te - tay
Beer - Cerveza - thur-vey-sah
Water - agua - ag-wah
Red wine - vino rojo - vee-no row-hoe
Wine - vino Tinto - vee-no tin-toe
Lemonade - limonada - limon-ard-ah
Coffee with Milk - Cafe con leche
Food

Tomato - Pomodoro - pomm-oh-door-oh

Hamburger - hamburguesa - ham-bur-gey-sah

Subway style sandwich / baguette - Bocadillo - Bock-ah-dee-yo

Omelette style cake (served cold) - Quesadilla - Kay-sah-dear

Croissant - Croissant - Kwa-sont

Could I have this ...(item)... please - Punga may eso ... (item you point to on menu) por favor - Pun-gar may esso ... (item)... pour favv-oar.

Chicken - pollo - po-yo

Example sentences

I want a table for one / two people - Quiero uno mesa para uno / dos personas - Key-air-oh ooh-no maysa para ooh-no / doss pear-sown-ahs

Please could I have a beer - Quisiera uno cerveza por favor - key-see-air-ah ooh-no ther-vay-sa pour favv-oar

Where is the Camino? Donde esta el camino? - Don-day est-ah el ca-me-no

Where are the toilets? - Donde estan los servicios? - Don-day est-ann los ser-bee-theo-s?

Do you speak English? - Habla Ingles? - ab-la in-gless?

Please can I have some water - Quiseira Agua por favor - Key-see-ear-rah agwa pour fav-oar

How much is this? - Quanto questa - kwon-tah quest-ah?

Could I please have a lemonade? - Queseira uno limonada por favor - Key-see-ear-rah ooh-no limon-arda pour favv-oar

Hostels

Landlord - Hospitalero - hospital-air-oh

Fire escape - escalara mecanica - escal-air-ah mechanic-ah

Stairs - escalara - es-cal-air-ah

Hot and cold taps

hot - caliente - cal-ee-ent-ay

cold - frio - free-oh

Two beds please - Dos Camas Por Favor - Doss cam-ass pour fave-oar

Boots - Botas - boat-ahs (usually found in each hostel, where you all put your muddy boots).

Walking Sticks - bastones - bas-tons (like tongs) (Usually you will see a sign Botas y Bastones, in a room where you would have your boots and walking sticks. This is why it's a good idea to have your initials written on the back of your boots, and tieing your sticks together with a caribina.

Simple phrases

Where is the toilet? - Donde este el baño? - Don-day esta el banyo?

Please - por favv-oar

Do you have a bed? - Tienes uno cama - tea-en-ease ooh-no cam-ah

Thanks for everything - gracias por todos - grass-ee-ahs pour toe-dose

Pilgrim - peregrino - pe-re-green-oh

Walk - caminar - cam-in-ah

Coffee with milk - cafe con leche - ca-fay con lech-ay

Coffee without milk - cafe sin leche - ca-fay sin lech-ay

Coffee without milk - cafe negro - ca-fay neh-row

How much us this? - Quanto es?

Breakfast - Desayuno - deh-say-oo-no

I would like a Lemonade please - Queseira uno Limonada / Kas Limon por favor - kay-see-era ooh-no limon-arda / Kass Limon pour favv-oar

I would like a coffee with milk - Queseira un cafe con leche - kay-see-era un cafe con le-chay pour favv-oar

Could I have this ...(item)... please - Punga may eso ... (item you point to on menu) por favor - Pun-gar may esso ... (item)... pour favv-oar.

Please could I have the bill - La Quenta porfavor - La kwenta pour favv-oar

Pharmacy - Farmacia - Far-ma-theeya (like the in theo)

I have a blister - Tengo uno poyar - ten-go ooh-no poy-ah (point at your foot).

Do you have a Stamp? (for your pilgrims passport) - Tengo uno sello? - ten-go ooh-no sayo (make an action of a stamp on your pilgrim passport).

Donation - Donativo - don-at-ee-voh

I am lost (man) - Estoy perdido - es-toy pear-dee-doh

I am lost (woman) - Estoy perdida - es-toy pear-dee-dah

Where is the Camino? - Dónde está el camino? - Donday esther el ca-meen-oh

Of course, if you wish to learn more, then I highly recommend the AA Phrasebook Spanish ISBN 978-0-7495-6031-7 or check out the videos on Youtube, or Duolingo, if you want to go a bit more indepth.

DAILY ROUTINE

Every single day is different on the Camino, but to make things easier and ensure we had a bed for the night (because Albergues soon get booked up), we soon settled into a routine.

We structured our Day roughly as follows.
 5:25am: wake up
 5:30am: pack our sleeping bags, and kits in the dark, quietly and without torches to prevent waking others up.
 6:00am: leave the dorms, and the Albergue (hostel) and start walking in the dark using head torches, following the Camino arrows.
 8:00am: arrive at a village and eat breakfast (usually a croissant and coffee or something similar).
 12:00pm: - ish - Stop for lunch.
 Walk until 2:00pm to ensure we had a place to sleep.
 2:00pm-ish:
 - Arrive at Albergue.
 - Pay for Albergue
 - Put boots in locker / on communal boot shelf

- Karen would go for a shower while I wrote my journal and looked after our stuff.
- I would go for a shower while Karen looked after our stuff and she would write her journal.
- We would wash our clothes together
- We would sleep until 6:00pm-ish (everything is closed because everyone takes Siesta in Spain between 2:00pm and 7:00pm (even schools close)).

7:00pm: We would walk around the local area, perhaps meet up with people

8:00pm: Eat a pilgrims' meal (typically something with high protein and carbs (steak and chips and some red wine).

10:00pm: Back to the Albergue to write more journal and sleep.

It was a fantastic experience, something I will never forget.

PRACTICE WALK
15TH MARCH 2019

Hardwick Ford, Clumber Park, Yorkshire.

As we were living in Yorkshire, we went out on some practice walks. This sounded like a good idea in theory, and the walks were lovely. It meant that we could try out our shoes, packs, and sticks, and hopefully get some sort of feel of what it would be like, going up and down hills in the Yorkshire Dales.

However, the Yorkshire Dales are minor bumps compared with the mountainous countryside of France and Spain.

Diary entry by Brett

Today, Karen and I took a nice steady walk, wearing our hiking gear and carrying rucksacks. It was a steady pace at roughly 3mph over 10 miles and we managed it in 3 hours, 40 minutes.

Along the way, we stopped to take some photos.

The start of the walk, a chance to use the selfie stick, and try out our boots, and rucksacks.

Halfway around our walk, we stopped and took in the scenery. It was such a beautiful sight to behold.

Time for a quick picture before we go home.

TRAVELLING TO FRANCE - DAY 1
29TH APRIL 2019

Rotherham (Near Sheffield in the UK) to Biarritz (France) - Day 1 of travelling.
The weather was sunny.

Our Itinerary was quite simple.
3 Trains to the airport.
07:17 - Rotherham Central to Doncaster.
08:14 - Doncaster to Peterborough.
09:06 - Peterborough to Stansted Airport.
1 short flight to Biarritz.
14:05 - Flight to Biarritz - FR372 - Arrived 17:05
Hotel: Premiere Classe Biarritz
1 night. Check in: 4pm to 9pm.
Checkout before 11am next day.

Diary entry by Brett.

Well, what a day!! Last night we went to bed early to make sure we slept well, as we knew we would travel most of today. Unfortunately, that didn't work out. After sweltering temperatures, we both woke up at 4am. So, we got ourselves dressed and walked to the railway station. Several hours and 3 train changes later, we arrived at the airport.

A few hours later and a security concern over Karen's kindle and some weird non-existent liquid in my backpack showing up on the security monitor, we were onboard the jet to Biarritz.

After a short flight, we landed several hours later and spotted a few Camino'ers. I wonder if we meet them along the way?

After getting out of the airport, someone asked us for directions in French... thankfully, they were asking where the airport was, so I just used my high school French, and when that didn't work, I pointed towards it.

We got to our hotel, dumped our bags, changed our shoes, loaded our mini rucksacks with valuables, and after a 2-mile walk to town, we stopped for some food by the beach. I grabbed my crocs, put them on, and ended up with blisters straight away. So, I applied some blister plasters, and bought a pair of flip-flops, and we both ate burgers and ice cream on the beach. How ironic, we did all the research and training. We haven't even got to St.Jean Pied-de- port and I've got two blisters already.

Meanwhile, Karen is feeling a little poorly because of travelling. The air pressure popped her ears, and she doesn't seem to have felt right since. Hopefully, this will pass.

Tomorrow, we are off to St.Jean Pied-de-port and picking up our pilgrim passports.

Diary entry by Karen.

Had an interesting day. Made all of our connections well, and in good time. Walked into Biarritz to see the beach and have some food. We need to sort out some footwear for Brett, got blisters from crocs and flip-flops.

The hotel is very basic, but pleasant and at least we got to share a double bed for the last time for several days.

Karen stood next to the beach at Biarritz

Our Plane.

The sand is lovely. We stopped on the beach and ate ice cream.

TRAVELLING TO FRANCE - DAY 2
30TH APRIL 2019

Biarritz (France) to St.Jean Pied-de-port - Day 2 of travelling.

The weather was sunny.

Our Itinerary was quite simple.

2 Trains from Biarritz to St.Jean Pied-de-port.

11:00 - Biarritz (SNCF TER 866472) to Bayonne 11:15

11:54 Bayonne (SNCF TER 867307) to St.Jean Pied-de-port 12:53

Hostel: Hostel Gite Zuharpita.

Diary entry by Brett.

We got up around 8ish, packed up, went to the reception of the hotel, and the lady let me keep the hotel keycard as a souvenir, which I stuck in my journal. After a short walk to the Gare de Biarritz (Biarritz Railway Station), Karen and I had a cup of tea and a muffin, then jumped on an SNCF train to St. Jean Pied-de-port.

A short walk to the railway station and a train to Bayonne. After that, there was a small wait, and another train, this time, to our last destination for this journey and the start of our next St.Jean pied-de-port. Woohoo!!

On the train, some ladies from Florida sat next to us and talked about how they walk everywhere. They thought we were bonkers for only having 2 sets of clothing. Everyone got off the train wearing backpacks.

By the way, my blisters are healing nicely, but after all that walking today, my muscles hurt in places I didn't even know they could hurt. Tomorrow we walk across the Pyrenees (1 mile climb, 20 mile walk). If the weather is good, we hope to have some gooooood pictures.

Diary entry by Karen.

Travelled by train to St.Jean Pied-de-Port. Had a photo, went and bought equipment. Got Credential (Pilgrim Passport) and had a lovely lunch (ham baguette and tea). Looked around and went to a couple of supermarkets, and got the lay of the land. Feeding ourselves is going to be fun. As soon as we got here, you can tell it's Camino orientated. Everyone getting off the train with backpacks. Bumping into people in shops. Some can speak French, and others laughing their way through transactions. We have bought lunch for tomorrow, and all is well. Pizza for tea.

More by Brett

After a short walk to the pilgrims office, we bought our pilgrims passports (also known as credentiale, proof that we are doing the Camino, which you must have to get into the hostels) and this included our first stamp. Each place you go to must give you a stamp to prove you have stayed there. Once you have a stamp, you are not allowed to return to that albergue (hostel) and must continue moving forward on your journey.

With passports in hand, we walked to our first hostel, just around the corner. This place was only small, just 20 beds, and Karen and I had to take our shoes off. They then showed us to our beds.

After filling our small backpacks with our valuables, we changed into our shoes and went outside. The views were simply breathtaking. We ate a lovely lunch (Ham baguette and a cup of tea). Some time later, we found ourselves at a supermarket, filling our backpacks with supplies for tomorrow's walk across the Pyrenees Mountains.

Apples, bananas, sun cream and sandwiches.

We finished the day with a walk to a pharmacy, and more supplies from a supermarket, then went for a pizza.

Getting off the train, everyone had backpacks and wanted to take pictures

The view from the train on the way to St.Jean Pied de Port.

Our first Camino arrow.

One of the many bridges in St. Jean Pied de Port.

OUR CAMINO DIARY - DAY 1
1ST MAY

St.Jean to Burgette. (28.1km)

Diary entry by Brett.

Today was an earrrrrrly start. Woke up at 5:30 and tried our best to pack up as quiet as possible, and all was going well, until someone switched the light on and blinded everyone, then someone else shouted out "good morning pilgrims" and we all made as much noise as we liked, lol

We set out in the dark and travelled a loooooooong way, up the town and into the mountains of the Pyrenees (I should have packed a spare pair of knees, pfft).

Karen put up with a lot of complaining from me because I was so slow and constantly in pain, stretching muscles I didn't even know existed.

We met a few people, and that helped international relations, haha. Every step we took, we spurred each other on and we walked and walked and .... walked.

We stopped at Orrisson for some breakfast (tortilla and basque cake (tasted like Bakewell tart) which we both really enjoyed).

Finally, after 1 mile up and 20 miles across, through many types of terrain (including snow) we finally arrived at our destination - Roncesvalles (pronounced Ron-sir-vai-ess) - a beautiful place and asked for 2 beds. Sadly, however... the Albergue at Roncesvalles was full, and we had to walk two more kilometres to Burgette to get somewhere to sleep.

Burgette was also full! But we were told that there was an emergency hostel at the sports hall (all the other hostels were full too) and finally found a large bare, echoey hall with concrete floors and wooden benches. The man in charge said they said they are bringing blankets and probably mattresses.

The Cruz Rojo (Spanish Red Cross) arrived with blankets and fold up beds, and the press arrived too.

Good news - no new blisters

Bad news we both ache everywhere else lol

Diary entry by Karen

Today was a long day. The climb to Orrison was the worst. But the bask cake was amazing and tasted great. It was lovely going over the Pyrenees. Brett seemed to suffer from the climb and going down. It took us 12.5 hours, leaving at 6:30am and getting to Roncesvalles at 7pm. We were told they were full and so we had emergency accommodation in a Sports Hall with no light. It was cold, and I had a bad toothache. The emergency staff arrived with camp beds and blankets.

Although it was a tough day, we felt God had provided for our basic needs. We were the last to wake up to emergency staff taking down the beds.

This picture is of Karen and I stood on the cattle grid which marks the France to Spain border, and the structure behind us, is a solar powered Wi-Fi hotspot... on top of a mountain. While walking across the mountain, I got a spam phone call asking if I had been involved in an accident... I replied, 'not yet, but I might, if I don't hang up' then hung up, to make sure I didn't fall down the mountain. Haha.

This is the top of the mountain. On the right, you can see snow, but you can also see Karen with her t-shirt on. It was roasting hot, and the snow was still there. This experience was very surreal.

Although it was a tough day, we felt God had provided for our basic needs. We have beds! The police brought the Cruz Rojo (Red Cross), who bought some fold up beds, and blankets. A camera crew even came along, because of the record number of Pilgrims walking the Camino this year. We might be on Television.

OUR CAMINO DIARY - DAY 2
2ND MAY

Burgette to Zubiri (18.8km)

Diary entry by Brett

Today we met lots of people - bumped into a few we already recognise, and started creating nicknames for them, to make it easier to remember who they are. Among them are Miss Texas, Kim from Australia, Donna from Florida, Fiachra from Ireland, and his friend Seamus, who went to Pamplona full of blisters. We started our morning with breakfast at the Ederbena Taberna for some croissant, Basque cake, and tea.

We then walked 13 miles through rocky terrain up and down from wooded trails and forty-five degree bladed jagged rocks - heavy going, and very difficult to walk on. We arrived at Zubiri and bumped into Miss Texas, who had been waiting for two hours outside on a cold step (sunny but icy wind) who told us all albergues (hostels) in Zubiri are full.

We then went to a cafe and had pepperoni pizza, a cup of tea, and a strange coffee with milk sweet. We found that there was another sports hall available, and there was a wait before it would be opening.

Karen and I went for a walk to pass the time, and got some paracetamol for the pain in my shoulders, knees, calves and ankles. When you see a sign along the Camino, it might say 5km... but it doesn't tell you it will be rocky, hilly, or go upwards and downwards all the time.

We went into a bar (Spanish cafe) and found some hot chocolate (literally like a melted chocolate bar in a mug) and got warm.

In the sports hall, we all handed out foam mattress-style bedding to sleep on (Karen and I slept on the same foam) and other slept on wooden boxes after (with carpet on them) we had run out of foam (8 pieces between 20 of us).

We then found the showers and got cleaned, and changed our clothes (first time in 4 days). The sports hall floodlights were switched on all night, with no chance to switch them off.

Diary entry by Karen

Another interesting day. We awoke this morning to the emergency team taking down the beds and finding out we were the only ones left, (tip need to set alarm lol).

We were on the road for 7.30am and all was going well. The last 5km getting into Zubiri was tough going, and the ground looked like stone that looked like something had ploughed it strangely at a 45-degree angle. We met a lady called Donna from Florida and one from Australia, and two crazy lads from Ireland. We have had a fab day even though we all had bad news on arrival. Night two, still not enough beds.

We had to decide to either stay at Zubiri in a sports hall that had lights and a shower (better than the night before) or take a taxi to Pamplona. We stayed here. The camaraderie here is amazing. We want to walk the entire distance if we can, and everyone is clubbing together and saying that it's all part of the Camino experience.

Thought of the day by Karen.

Today has been about realising that we all travel at different speeds, the speed and the distance don't matter. What matters is enjoying the moment. We walked across amazing stepping stones today and sat by a well to enjoy a snack and the peace. We were walking in a wood that was high above the highway. Absolutely amazing that such beauty and peace can be in harmony alongside such busyness and noise.

The sports hall at Zubiri, where we slept on pieces of foam. It was freezing cold, and we only had 8 pieces of foam between 20+ of us, and the floodlights stayed on all night. One Man had no blankets, and wouldn't accept one. We assumed he wanted the full Pilgrim experience.

Mindless graffiti or motivational support? It says "Fight all the hatred of the world, with Love".

This bridge (square concrete posts about 1 metre apart) was trickier to cross than it looks, especially with walking poles. Each Square also had a large gap between, which meant that we risked falling off the blocks, and into the water.

OUR CAMINO DIARY - DAY 3
3RD MAY

Zubiri to Villava (16.1km)

Diary entry by Karen

Today we set the alarm and woke before it (5.30) . We planned to stay for breakfast in the next town to find it all closed. We got breakfast at 9.30, which was very nice. It was wet today with drizzly rain, but we still had a fab time.

I had an idea of going to a hostel off the path to a place called Huarte. I thought others wouldn't bother to walk the extra 1km, but it was closed, so we had to walk to the next town, Villava. We are in a lovely hostel with showers, heating, washing machine etc.. we are having the pilgrim meal for the first time today (mixed salad, tender turkey with fries, yogurt with red berries, bread and red wine).

Diary entry by Brett

We woke up at 5.30pm, and noticed our Irish friend had been given some blankets (he had refused the offers of our sleeping bags several times, and we were glad he was now warmer in this freezing cold hall). We had trouble sleeping because the floodlights for the sports hall were on all night and no-one came with beds or blankets, so Karen and I stayed together on 1 piece of foam.

We left the concejo de Zubiri in complete darkness. It was cold, and I was glad I have my wooly hat with built in torch. We walked by the magnesium factory and carried on through farmland. It was a lot easier-going today, quite flat, and we had to look out for trucks and walking signs as we passed the magnesium quarry.

After lots of pretty woodland walks, we tried to find an albergue off the beaten track and passed a beautiful waterfall, and more woodland. Unfortunately it was closed, so we carried on to the next town for breakfast, Jaffa cake type pancake, and some tortilla with cafe con leche (coffee with milk). Karen had a pork baguette and black tea - muy bien (very good). We carried onwards through town after town (hamlet) and pretty fields to a deserted hamlet built into a rock-face.

More woodlands, a water stop, past a beautiful church, then through subways adorned with graffiti and a stop at Huarte supermarket for supplies (sweets, etc).

We met a funny man called Dan with a peacock, and donation stand, so grabbed some rocket fuel coffee and carried on miles later, eventually arriving at Villava, and found the albergue.

We were able to wash our clothes, woohoo! It had rained most of today, and we were just glad to be clean, warm and dry.

Thought of the day by Karen

How we are blessed - on the walk today we were halfway up a cliff edge after a staggering climb to amazing views, we turned a corner and there was a man in a barn serving coffee, tea, and orange juice with such a welcoming smile and saying hello to everyone. He was raising money for a charity and everything was by donation.

He joked about being a cowboy and how this peacock in the barn was his horse, amazing hospitality

After such a climb, it was an unexpected nice blessing.

I wonder how many blessings do we fail to notice?

The magnesium factory, early in the morning. We walked along with our head torches on, and had to be careful of trucks from the factory, and the quarry.

We had a mixed salad with turkey, fries and yoghurt with berries (I forgot to photograph the salad)

The tame peacock who was with the funny man selling coffee for donations

OUR CAMINO DIARY - DAY 4
4TH MAY

Villava to Pamplona (4.7km) - Rest Day in Pamplona

Diary entry by Karen

We have had a rest day, as such, today. After walking 4km into Pamplona, we arrived at 9:30am so have had a great day looking around the shops, going to the tourist sights and seeing what's going on. There were street performers (two marching bands) and a big 'stop bullying' campaign in the plaza with lots of activities for children.

We ate at Burger King, and for the evening we bought a frozen meal (It was horrible!).

We noticed all pilgrims were invited to a free guided tour of the Cathedral and some services. So we went into the shared prayers afterwards, which were lovely. The last few days have been about walking, aching muscles and blisters. It was nice to have some space for reflection.

Another good day

Diary entry by Brett

After a breakfast at the albergue of toast and

marmalade, with a choice of coffee or orange juice, we took a short walk to Pamplona.

Thought of the day

At the shared prayer service, they gave us a copy of the pilgrims' beatitudes. The lines will take some days to reflect upon, but it's beautiful.

As part of the service, we were able to share anything and one lady said, that the Camino was a world family. We have found that to be true, too. That people, regardless of nationality or anything else, talk to each other, share stories and help each other.

I wonder if, when you take away everyone's security blankets, and they are left with a backpack (carrying all that they have) lends itself to this common experience, and the knowledge of leaning on each other and God.

Our hostel door and the scroll outside it.

The inside of the dorms, we are in bunk beds again :)

Pamplona cathedral That's Tomorrow is another gruelling journey up and down a small mountain towards Puenta la Reina - if our already swollen feet make it that far... for now, more sleep. Good night :)

OUR CAMINO DIARY - DAY 5
5TH MAY

Pamplona to Puente La Reina (23.8km)

Post by Brett

They say you don't walk the Camino; the Camino walks you. Today proved that. We set off early (6am) from our albergue in Pamplona and walked uphill. Through stoney footpaths, my left foot was still swollen but no pain. Instead, my right knee felt like someone poked a dart in it, and I have pain with every step. This didn't stop us today as we walked through woodland, farmland, and up to the top of the mountain.

We got a hostel, woohoo. For tea we had paella with chicken. It tasted completely different to the one we make at home.

After washing our clothes by hand, and hanging them to dry, we sat in the garden for a while, and chatted to a man called Johannes from the Netherlands.

Thought for the day by Karen

Two things today.

1. As we were coming up a side of a hill come mountain heading to Alto de Perdon, a man walked past and raised his hands in the air saying "gracias Dios" (which means "thank you God"). It was a lovely moment of thanking God for his garden that he created. Later in the day, I was reminded of this by some wild flowers on the pathway.

2. We got lost leaving this morning, learnt how to read the signs and helped a Dutch man learn how to read the signs. So today I have helped someone to find the right way and as part of the trail you follow the person in front of you, watching where they put their feet, which is a nicer surface etc... it's a time of following the right way, be it making sure you're on the right path and making sure you're on the right surface. How good are we in everyday life at helping others to follow the right path? Either with their work, or hobbies, techniques etc.. or faith?

With a bitter crosswind, we were lucky we didn't get blown over, and we were both glad we had our buffs! Eventually, we arrived at Puente La Reina (The Queens Bridge) and found a beautiful albergue with many facilities for only 5 euros.

The view from the top of Alto de Perdon. We could see for miles, and miles.

The famous iron cut outs of the pilgrims at the top of the mountain.

OUR CAMINO DIARY - DAY 6
6TH MAY

Puente La Reina to Estella (21.9km)

Post by Brett

A relatively easier day up and down 3 hills from Puente la Reina to Estella, we stopped at a small baker on the way up one hill and had the most amazing croissants, then carried on making it in good time to shower and walk around the area. All in all, a good day. My blisters are no longer a problem. Karen has one or two, which she is treating, and I have just bought a knee support. Hopefully, the twinge won't bother me now. More tomorrow when we head for Los Arcos (we hope, lol).

Diary Entry by Karen

Today was an easier day, walking through farm fields of olive groves and vineyards. Most of the journey was on farm tracks. One highlight of today was coming into "The Olive Garden" an amazing rest area that is being developed for Pilgrims. We are walking, using the John Brierley guide to the Camino de Santiago, at the moment and getting into Estella at approximately 2-2:30pm.

Thought of the day by Karen

Today, as we were walking along the farm tracks, we came to a sign that said "Paradise under construction". A lovely bit of paradise as a rest area; amazing! It reminded me that where we live is paradise under construction and we can all do our bit to make it a better place by the things we say and do. It will be fully constructed when Jesus comes again. How amazing?

Walking up to "The Olive Garden," we saw a sign that gave us the chance to rest.

We sat and had a welcomed rest from the heat and tiredness. The shade was welcoming, and the greenery showed us just how well looked after this place was.

A chance to take off our backpacks and rest under some shade, and sit on the chairs they had built out of wood.

OUR CAMINO DIARY - DAY 7
7TH MAY

Estella to Los Arcos (21.5km)

Diary entry by Brett

Today was quite a long day, although it was easy-going on foot. 13 miles of gentle up and down along gravel roads, paths, through beautiful scenery, and to the wine fountain. The small dribble of wine I drank left me feeling quite euphoric. Our new Camino friends Johannes, Shelley and Doug (from America), and the Australian couple, along with Miss New Zealand, seem to walk at the same pace, as we all arrived in the same towns, meeting up with each other, and sometimes booking the same albergues. Tonight Shelley and Doug were due to be in our four-bed room, but stayed with friends instead, so Karen and I had bunk beds in the room to ourselves. We arrived at our hostel, and rested for a few hours, while the rest of Spain took a siesta, then went out for tea. Tomorrow is likely to be a long slog, as we walk the 18 miles to Logroño, so we need to rest as well as we can. I've lost my kindle, either whilst out and about, or back in the dorm. It's got all my reading books and Camino maps on it.

Diary entry by Karen

Today was probably the easiest walking terrain. Mostly farm tracks and pretty flat. The scenery kept changing, which kept our interest. We arrived at the wine fountain at 7am expecting it to be closed, but it wasn't. Brett tasted the wine and we took some photos.

Arrived at the Albergue at 1pm, the earliest so far, and we seem to be getting stronger as the days go by. We had to get a knee brace yesterday for Brett, which really helped today.

Tomorrow we have some decisions to make. We can either have a short day and stay at Vianna, or an 18 mile day, and walk to Logroño. We will let you know tomorrow what we decided. The food here is amazing

Thought of the day by Karen

We have had the same routine so far on this trip. We get up about 5.30am, leave 6am, walk to the recommended stop and then shower, wash clothes, go for a wander, stay out till tea time 7pm and then go back to sleep. Here the siesta is 3pm - 6-7ish so while we are walking around nothing is open.

Today we did all we had to do, and then rested through siesta and went out for a wonder at 6pm, looked round a beautiful church, the town and had tea.

It is hard for me to rest, but this trip is teaching me how to rest, to refresh, to have time reading etc. At the moment, I am sitting on a bed ready for what's next.

I wonder how often we run on half empty when, if we took time to rest for awhile, we would run on full?

The entrance to Azquerta, a beautiful village where we had breakfast

The wine fountain - left tap for red wine, right tap for water

The wine fountain - left tap for red wine, right tap for water

OUR CAMINO DIARY - DAY 8
8TH MAY

Los Arcos to Logroño (27.8km)

Post by Brett

Are we mad? Read on to find out more.

Today was long, hard (although not as hard as the first day across the Pyrenees), windy (a gale of warm wind with lots of dust), but rewarding.

After getting up early and struggling to get out of the albergue (hostel), I struggled mentally for a while because my kindle was missing this morning, and that meant I couldn't do our daily reading (or look through the Camino maps I had installed on my kindle), so I read from my phone instead.

Karen found the magic button to the albergue gates (which completely eluded the rest of the Pilgrims) and once opened we were soon on our way.

We walked from approx 7am and came across the next village, then had breakfast at approx 9am (croissants and a drink). The weather was overcast, and at one moment, it rained. The idea was to head to Vianna (18.3k from Los

Arcos) and if we felt strong enough after lunch, to carry on to Logroño (11.5km) and up and down through dusty blasts of nonstop wind through fields, wooded areas and other points of interest, with no water stops for 12k.

After finally arriving at Logroño (5pm, walking for approx 9 hours through humid heat and blasts of wind), we booked into an albergue and had a rest for an hour before heading into town for a look around. This place is huuuuu- uuuge !!! We stopped to eat at a kebab house, it was fab :)

More tomorrow, do we go to Navarrete (13k) and get a place in an association, (whatever that is) or carry on to Najera (28k lol, we must be mad) and go to a donativo (a humble place with few facilities but more "pilgrimy")?

Let's see tomorrow when we have rested and know what the weather is like.

Diary entry by Karen

Today, we weren't sure how far we would walk. It was potentially our longest day of 18.3 miles. The terrain, for most of the day, was good. The damper to the day was that Brett lost his kindle last night. This has made us a bit more vigilant.

When we got to Vianna, Brett was determined to make it to Logroño, so we had lunch, a large break, and then walked through strong winds to Logroño. It took us until 5pm-ish, but we made it. A great sense of achievement. Logroño (which is the capital of the Rioja region) is smaller than I expected. We had a good wander and enjoyed a kebab.

Thought of the day by Karen

Today everyone was looking at the guide at breakfast after walking 4km and saying the next bit is tough, it had a descent of 10%. We were not looking forward to this dangerous part and, at the descent sign, we had a water stop. If I was at home, I would clean or have a cuppa. The descent was not as bad as we thought. It had several curves in it that made it easier. When we got to the bottom, we decided it hadn't been that bad at all.

We build things and tasks up so big that they become a source of worry or stress. Tasks or things we have to complete tend not to be as bad as we think they are going to be. Instead of procrastinating, take heart, take courage and just do it. You will feel relieved afterwards.

One of the cool Camino signs (a Camino shell).

Logroño Cathedral

Some graffiti is actually good :) This "artwork" tells us there are 616km left to Santiago, and even wishes us a Buen Camino.

OUR CAMINO DIARY - DAY 9
9TH MAY

Logroño to Najera (28.9km)

Diary entry by Brett

Another long day of pathways and road for about eighty percent of our journey. We met a lovely old peasant pilgrim called Marciano on our journey from Logroño (7:30am) to Navarette. We stopped for some breakfast. Later we ate lunch (12.9k) and carried on walking to Najera (18.5k) arriving at our albergue completely exhausted at roughly 4:30pm.

We had some interesting stops along the way, meeting Marciano, and a visit to the parroquial church of Navarette, Tomorrow is likely to be the same, and we are going to need lots of water (thank goodness I packed the camelpak water bladder in the backpack).

Diary entry by Karen

Today was a lovely start through a fabulous park,

around a lake, and through woodland, extremely picturesque, into Navarette. On the way was a donativo (small stand with some stuff for sale - donate what you want) that was special. I bought a postcard. We had coffee and cake.

The walk after that wasn't pretty, so it felt like a slog. We got to the albergue at about 4pm, and both of us felt shattered. We haven't really explored because of tiredness, but we have had the best hamburger ever. Time for an early night.

The blessing today is that we are staying at a donativo and the dormitory is bunk beds with 2 bunks together. They have allocated us a bottom bunk next to each other and tried to keep all couples together so you are not sleeping literally next to a stranger

THOUGHT of the day by Karen

Today, one stop we had was at Navarette . We visited a beautiful church there. The altar was spectacular and extremely opulent. I don't like this sort of thing, but I understand the sentiment. People want to make God's house as beautiful as possible as a way of showing their love, devotion, and as an act of faith.

I wonder what we do to show God how important he is to us through love, devotion and faith?

Inside the Church in Navarette.

OUR CAMINO DIARY - DAY 10
10TH MAY

Najera to Santo Domingo de la Calzada (21.3km)

Diary entry by Brett

Today, while we wanted to walk all the way to Hospital San Juan Baptista, our feet just wouldn't let us. So, we braved the wind once again along dusty gravel roads and ended up in Santo Domingo at another albergue municipal. First thoughts (as someone struggled with their reservation) were to leave and go to the monastery, but we paid our money and walked up two flights of stairs to the Grañon Suite (the closest we got to Grañon so far).

We dumped our bags and boots and headed off out to get some food. Our 18k day has only taken us just under six and a half hours, woohoo!

Tomorrow, who knows where God will take us. We ate lunch and relaxed before washing clothes and went out later. After a quick look around the area, we went for tea at the same place we ate lunch. The British guy who was there really upset the waiter by deliberately taking up a table for four people.

I ordered steak and chips (the biggest steak I have ever seen). It took up 2/3rds of the plate, and there was just enough room for egg and chips. After tea, we visited the Santa Iglesia Cathedral of Santo Domingo de la Calzada and got to see the skull of Santo Domingo, then went down into the crypt where there are most amazing mosaics and the tomb of Santo Domingo himself.

This cathedral is the home to some chickens and the bar from the gallows where legend tells, that a pilgrim boy was hanged for a week but didn't die. In the story, the parents told the man in charge that their son was alive. His reply was, he is alive as the roast chickens on my plate... and with that; the chickens got up, and walked off the plate. The son was pulled down, and two chickens and the handmans wooden bar, now reside in the cathedral as a reminder of that day. We then went to the festival (1000 years of Saint Domingo, and I bought some souvenirs to make the occasion).

DIARY ENTRY by Karen

Today was a shorter walk day, and we arrived at 12.30pm but we were tired. The rash on my legs is causing some issues, but all part of the journey. We talked for some time with Gary and Sue from Australia. It is a special day in Santo Domingo. It's 1000 years since the death of Domingo. An amazing life of not being able to do what he wanted but doing something God inspired. He dedicated his life to the pilgrims, building hospitals, bridges, and a church that is now the Cathedral. He is reported to have done miracles. It was a complete party atmosphere that we got caught up in. Brilliant Day.

THOUGHT of the day by Karen

We arrived upon a fiesta celebrating Santo Domingo, and it's a remarkable story. This man wanted to join the clergy, but because of his lack of learning, he wasn't allowed. Instead, he dedicated his life to the pilgrims on the Camino. He created a pilgrims' hospital and built a church here that is now the cathedral. It's an amazing life that was dedicated to helping people and to serving God, even though it wasn't his first choice.

Sometimes the bigger picture that God can see, is better than what we could ever think or dream. So when you are discouraged with your plan, look for God's plan, usually it's better.

Karen filling up with drinking water from one of the many pilgrim taps.

Our Camino Diary - Day 10

Statue of Santo Domingo

These push around bulls were squirting the children with water, and the children would use a rag to "enrage the bull". The entire square was thumping with music, but we had to watch out for pickpockets.

OUR CAMINO DIARY - DAY 11
11TH MAY

Santo Domingo de la Calzada to Belorado

DIARY ENTRY by Brett

Today was pretty boring, a reasonably quick route (only 22k). We had to stop for me to change into pairs of socks over the first 7km because my feet were on fire (think I may be allergic to the washing powder from the laundromat yesterday) but before the third pair of socks went on; I put on some antihistamine cream Karen bought a few days before for her hives.

And in more interesting news, we stumbled upon an amazing hostel (Albergue) which is more like a mini community complex. They have washing and drying facilities and an excellent restaurant, even a pool, for €6 each !!

Tomorrow's journey takes us towards San Juan de Ortega, but it's only got limited beds, so we may have to walk further.

. . .

Diary entry by Karen

Today the scenery wasn't great because of the misty rain. We walked 22km and came to the first albergue. The albergue was advertised as being out of town, but had a bar and restaurant. We needed a quiet day today with no sightseeing.

It is easily the best albergue we have stayed in yet,

Thought of the day by Karen

The weather was rubbish today and extremely misty, so no scenes to really look at. Therefore, time to think. Today I have been pondering on two different types of people. Those who get up early, and those who get to the albergues as quickly as possible. Watching them, I'm not sure they are taking in the scenery or what they are doing. We get overtaken by these all the time. We leave about the same time but we have a breakfast stop, coffee stop and lunch stop, so we arrive a couple of hours later with many pictures and thoughts about what we have seen.

I wonder if we sometimes can get so focused on the destination, the goal, completed; that we cannot notice the little blessings along the way. Today we walked through the village that was the birthplace of Santo Domingo. I wonder, how many people noticed?

The starter in our 3 course meal.

An entire bottle of wine for both of us (Karen drank a little too). Wine in Spain tastes so much fruitier, and they serve it chilled, which is definitely worth the experience!

An albergue with a swimming pool!

OUR CAMINO DIARY - DAY 12
12TH MAY

Belorado to St. Juan de Ortega (24.2km).

DIARY ENTRY by Brett

Yesterday's albergue was so good, we didn't want to get up. In fact, while some people left at half four, we gently woke up at 6am and were ready and packed by half six !!! What did we do today?

We went through three towns before we found one open for breakfast. Karen had a croissant she wasn't keen on, and I had bacon and eggs. After breakfast, we left the albergue, then walked, and walked, and walked! We went up and down a couple of hills (3060 ft at the highest) across many terrains, wooded paths, dusty trails, tarmac roads and rocky hills then found a nice little donation stall (donativo) where we were told that the next town was full (no beds) and she gave us a leaflet for her albergue instead. We walked on to the next town (San Juan de Ortega) and busting for the toilet, Karen went in a shop next to the monastery. While I looked after our rucksacks, I watched as a man went into the monastery (the only hostel in San Juan) and noticed he didn't come out. I put two and two together and asked if they had beds. So, we are currently staying in a monastery and this place is full of interesting and cool things.

Where are we going tomorrow? Not sure because we thought we might have to walk extra today and haven't really decided yet.

Diary entry by Karen

Today was an okay walk, but not that interesting. Beautiful views of the altos (hills) but a lot of track walking with trees on either side. The last 12km stretch seemed to go on forever. After being told that there would be no beds, we found some, so we stayed at the monastery.

We went to a pilgrims' mass, which was lovely and very much felt God. At the albergue, it was a communal meal, our first one. We met two lovely couples, one from Cantaloña and one from America.

Thought of the day by Karen

Today we did a lot of track walking with trees on both sides. We couldn't really see a view because of the trees.

One set of trees we passed was just showing signs of new life. We talked about how in the summer this would be an amazing shade for pilgrims. About 1000 metres on, we passed some evergreen trees that were providing shade now and several pilgrims were taking a rest.

It got me thinking, what are the constant things in our lives that will always be there, like the evergreen trees that will always provide shade and security for us i.e. family, spouse, children, faith, work etc... and what are those things that are just showing, those new possibilities that we are getting excited about i.e. a new adventure, planning a holiday, a new baby, a new opportunity.

Thank you, Lord, for all the things that are in our lives that are constantly giving us shade and security. Thank you also for the new things just beginning that have the potential to come to full blossom, those things that are exciting and surprising.

Amen

The monastery we stayed in.

Our Camino Diary - Day 12

Someone really liked the Camino, so they thought they would share with the word "love" and a heart shape. If you look really carefully, you can see it too.

Another day on the track. Today we saw wild orchids growing, they were beautiful.

OUR CAMINO DIARY - DAY 13
13TH MAY

St. Juan de Ortega to Burgos (26.1km).

Diary entry by Karen

Today was a mixture of terrain. The first few towns went by quickly as we walked and talked with our Argentinian Daniel, who we keep bumping into since day one. The last 12km was a tough walk through a park. It didn't seem to end, even though we kept seeing signs for the city of Burgos.

We had a little hassle trying to get into the apartment because of a communication problem. However, the apartment was very nice and a welcome break from being in a dorm with lots of people. It was nice to get a hot shower and to sleep in the same bed. We washed everything and got ready for the Meseta. We had a hamburger meal out with Daniel, the company, and the food was great.

Diary entry by Brett

Boy, what a day, lol

Today started with a bang... literally, as someone's sidebar fell off the top bunk of their bed and clattered with such an earth-shaking sound, it probably woke everyone in the whole albergue at 5:30am.

Shortly afterwards, while people packed, a crack in the door let light in, so someone switched on the lights, blinding everyone. With that, everyone packed. We started our walk from San Juan de Ortega to Burgos, picking up our boots and sticks on the way out of the albergue. Navigating our way back to the Camino was very easy compared to the last few days.

The first village we found was open (also a pleasant change compared to the last few days). We drank tea, ate chocolate pastries, and bumped into Johannes again and chatted. Then he walked on while we ate breakfast. We spoke to Daniel from Argentina (goatee man) and I ordered food and teas. The couple running the bar worked well together and were very entertaining. She sold me the pastries, and I had to walk upstairs to a small bar, where the man was receiving drinks orders left, right and centre.

While we walked, we chatted with Daniel some more. The man is close to retirement and reads in church as a lay reader. He told us he also goes to hospital and takes Holy Communion to people. He taught us a few words of Spanish and spoke to Karen about ecumenist ways.

Our second stop after rocky ground and me twisting my left ankle meant Daniel carried on, while we rested because of my injury. After several hours of walking, we arrived in Burgos.

As a part of the Camino, we had decided that rest days were essential, so pampered ourselves with a night in a hotel. When we arrived, we noticed the automated check-in machine outside the building was switched off. After a bit of detective work, (yay, for google and smartphones) we rang the hotel booking company, but my Spanish was not good enough to understand them, and we kept thinking they were talking about "hotel erotica" where we should check in. Karen checked her phone, and it said Hotel Boutique Musee on her banking app. Another quick Google and we found the place where we could talk to someone in person, and limped across town towards it.

When we arrived, the lady explained we were in the wrong place, and redirected to Hotel Via Gotika (not hotel erotica). Google maps came to the rescue again, and we limped back the same way we came, and found the diverted check-in place.

We queued, (noticing lots of people from the same hotel), and asked the lady to write instructions for check-in, so I could put them on the front door of the hotel. She obliged, stamping our credentials and we got the code for the building and the room number 101. Yay.

Arriving at the hotel, we punched in the door code, and walked into the lobby (a short corridor with a closed reception window, and some stairs), and found a phone at the desk. No-one works here. If you have a problem, you simply pick up the phone. We went up to room 101, and the room code they gave us didn't work. Argh.

Tired and frustrated (but seeing the funny side of it), I hobbled downstairs with Karen, and we rang them from the "24 hour manned reception" (phone in the lobby with closed reception) and was told that the room number was in fact 202, not 101.

We finally got in the room, and rested for a moment, then put our clothes in the washing machine, and Karen jumped into the shower. She got dressed while I showered, then I got out, put some trousers on, and began shaving.

The fire alarm went off! The fun never stops, haha.

With no shoes on, no shirt, and half a face full of shaving foam, we walked down the two flights of stairs to the "24 hour reception" while Karen, very concerned, shouted fire, to get people out to safety, only to find out... it was a false alarm! You seriously can't make this up. Crazy day or what?

After the neighbours explained they were cooking toast and the fire alarm went off, we all went safely back to our rooms and rested.

Later, we went for evening tea, and bumped into Daniel again. He ate with us again, (our treat this time). While we ate, he talked about Argentina and how expensive everything is in Spain. We toasted to the Camino, said goodnight to Daniel, and turned in for the night, in the luxury of our hotel suite, and watched The Big Bang Theory, all dubbed in Spanish.

Thought of the day by Karen

We are having a rest day today so we booked to stay in an apartment last night. We have our own bathroom with a hot shower, a mini kitchen, a washing machine, all basic stuff, but not shared with a hundred other people. The greatest gift, no snorers.

I wonder how much we take for granted in our lives. It's taken us two weeks of living in a dorm on bunk beds to appreciate a bed at a normal level, having a shower when we want to. What about the luxury stuff we have? Do we appreciate those things?

Thank you, Lord, for all that you have provided us with. We ask you to be with people who don't have the basics. Help us help them. Amen

The solitary parts of the Camino were the best places to reflect.

This is our "24 hour manned reception." A telephone on a shelf... in the locked lobby of the hotel.

OUR CAMINO DIARY - DAY 14
14TH MAY

Burgos - Rest Day.

Diary entry by Karen

Had a slow morning, having a lie-in and not getting up until 9-ish. Packed slowly and went for breakfast. Booked into the next albergue which is amazing and extremely modern. Going to do some sightseeing today.

We have looked around the cathedral, extremely grand. I loved the different altar fronts from different periods in history. Had to leave a little early, as Brett needed the toilet and then got himself locked out of the cathedral. We have had a lovely day off. Going to go to evening mass tonight and take some pictures of this amazing city. The mass was nice even though they didn't have any liturgy. It was good to be there and with your own relationship with God; and it gave a time for personal reflection. It made me wonder 'how welcoming are we to people coming into church? Do we make it easy for them to access our services? Do they feel welcome?'

Tea wasn't great, and I am learning not to eat red meat, need to have a look around first.

Diary entry by Brett

Today we got up lazily, watched a bit of TV and had a cuppa in bed. We left the hotel after packing rucksacks and tidying up. We started walking again, all the way from our hotel to the Albergue, and ate breakfast on the way. Walking near Burgos Cathedral we watched an open air children's concert. Booking into the albergue was a doddle, and the easy layout of the room surprised us. Each bunk has its own walkway, with a designated rucksack area next to your bunk. Each bunk also has its own light and electric socket. It almost feels like a very private room.

We dumped everything, made our bunks, and headed out for food. The Burger King has amazing stained glass windows. After lunch, we continued on to Burgos Cathedral and looked around the incredible building. Whilst paying for our "pilgrim special", we both received audio guides (which looked a bit like telephones).Each portion of the visit was numbered, and when we got to number 23, I had the sudden urge to use the toilet (the water in the cities simply wasn't agreeing with me), so I left Karen to continue looking around the cathedral, handed my telephone back to the receptionist (who was happy for me to come back without paying). and headed toward the talking toilets in the city square.

A moment or two later, I arrived back at the Cathedral, and was told by the security guard that the cathedral was closed at 4pm. I looked at my watch... 4:02pm :(I asked the security guard if I could wait for my wife, and she was happy that I could wait, but wasn't allowed to go inside... pfft.

I rang Karen and let her know where I was, and told her I was happy to wait outside while she finished her tour. 10 minutes later we met up, and headed towards the supermarket to grab some food for tomorrow's trip across the Meseta, and then went back to the albergue.

After a good rest, we went for mass, and they held it in a part of the cathedral that was a pilgrim only area. When that had finished, we ate tea. I had chicken, and Karen had ribs and roast potatoes.

AFTER ALL THE fun of yesterday, we are having a slower day looking round the cathedral in Burgos, I will post some pics later.

A stork's nest on top of a church (we've seen several already)

Burgos Cathedral

We took a selfie outside the back of Burgos cathedral, and got a great view looking downward onto the children singing in the square.

OUR CAMINO DIARY - DAY 15
15TH MAY

Burgos to Hornillas (21 km)

Post by Brett·

Today we left Burgos at around 6:40am (the doors were not unlocked until 6:30am) and ventured onward while the sun was still coming up.

Karen and I walked for about an hour, to the outskirts of Burgos, and onto the Camino trail.

More rocky road and gravelly pathways later, we found a small church in Rabe de los Calzados and investigated, using it as an excuse to get into the shade out of the heat. What we found inside was not only surprising, but very spiritual, too.

As well as the usual churchy stuff, some pictures, a few statues, pews and an altar, there was a lady who was stamping our pilgrim passports. While this is nothing new, what she did after stamping certainly was. On her right was a small rack with hundreds of string necklaces with a small pendant of stamped metal in the shape of Santa Maria, and after each pilgrim received their stamp, she would individually bless them and put a necklace over their heads. This was very emotional for some and very enlightening for others. When the nun blessed me, I said "Vaya Con Dios, Hermana De Christo" which means "Go with God, Sister of Christ." She seemed quite impressed with my Spanish. After the blessing, we headed out onto the Meseta (an endless stretch of land which goes on for approx 10 days with little shade or protection from the elements).

We walked, and it got hotter and higher, until eventually we came across a small town called Hornillas and had a look for a place to stay the night. The first three albergues were full, and as we geared up mentally to take on another 10k walk after today's (already walking 22k), I turned my head right to take a photo of a pretty church and then saw a sign for a very hidden municipal albergue as Karen was already down the road ahead of me.

I called her back; we looked in and got two beds, yay !!! After showering and washing our clothes, Karen rested while I went across the road to the bar / cafe and had a drink.

This little town doesn't offer a lot, but the hospitality is fantastic :)

Where are we going tomorrow? I haven't got a clue, but it will be day two of the meseta, so not much to take pictures of, probably.

Diary entry by Karen

Today we forgot to set the alarm, so woke up slightly later than intended. At 6:45am we were still walking, which is not bad. The first 10.4km was walked quickly, which shocked Brett. Then we stopped for a cuppa and a sandwich and headed into the Meseta.

We had a lovely experience in where we entered a church and received an individual pilgrims' blessing. There was this lovely lady who was stamping people's credentials and then giving them a small Santa Maria pendant to accompany them to Santiago. It was extremely moving, and many people left in tears. As we left, we saw bible quotes all over the side of other buildings. It was like the town wanted people to know there is a spiritual element to the pilgrimage.

It was in the right place, because as we left, we climbed into the Meseta. It wasn't a bad walk today. We both seem to be getting stronger as the days pass by. We have come to this lovely little village and although several albergues were "completo" (full) there were some spaces in the municipal, with the loveliest hostaleros (albergue owners) we have met.

THOUGHT of the day by Karen

Today we visited a church where a lovely lady was stamping people's credentials and individually blessing them. It was such a lovely moment and you couldn't help being touched whether you were a person of faith or not. There was no collection plate near her. It wasn't a gimmick, but a lovely moment that is a gift from the church. A few steps away is a side of a building that had some amazing bible quotes on.

From this we walked straight into the Meseta. We have finished the physical part of the Camino and this was a big bump into the mental part of the journey, reminding us we go with God.

Are we ready for the next part of the journey? Are you

ready for the next part of yours? Will we allow God to go with us?

The following photos mark the start of the Meseta.

The start of the meseta... 10 days of the same views, it is supposed to help you think.

The tiny church in Rabe de los Calzados. We entered, and joined a long queue, to wait, and be blessed by a nun.

These buildings mark the start of the Meseta.

Simply beautiful.

Karen being blessed by the nun. The whole experience, was very spiritual, and even more humbling.

Our Camino Diary - Day 15

This is a picture inside the little church.

The artwork is incredible.

The church I was taking a picture of which lead me to find the albergue we are now staying in.

The selfie at the top of the hill where we had lunch before heading down into Hornillas.

OUR CAMINO DIARY - DAY 16
16TH MAY

Hornillas to Castrojeriz.

Diary entry by Brett

We started off at about 5:30am today, getting dressed and packed, then downstairs for breakfast.

Breakfast was interesting, all laid out, with no sight of the hostalero. We walked into the room to find all the food and drinks prepared for us, and it soon became obvious that she had prepped it all the night before. People were microwaving their cold coffee in bowls, and the bread was slightly stale, even though it had been cling filmed.

We ate and left approx 6:20am to see the most incredible red sunrise. Over hill and valley we walked, with the odd stop here and there, for a cup of tea, water, etc.

As we approached the ruins of an old Abbey, a car donativo approached us. We bought a t-shaped cross, donating a euro in the basket, and he stamped our credential. The ruins were beautiful and very well looked after by nuns who were also blessing pilgrims. After a brief sit-down and a couple of pictures, we were on the road again. We bumped into our Camino friends Gary and Sue from Australia and soon got walking and talking.

Everything was going well until... I suddenly felt an intense pain in my forehead and a loud buzzing sound radiating through my skull, which just wouldn't go away, no matter how hard I shook my head. After dancing around like an idiot, ducking and wafting like a madman, with Karen wondering what on earth was going on, one of our Australian friends (Gary) shouted "he's got a black bee stuck to his head", at which point I realised what was going on, and after shaking a bit more, the bee released itself, leaving it's sting. Karen removed the sting and instantly applied the antihistamine cream (which she bought for her hives) to the sting area.

Panic over, we carried on walking through the town to our albergue (my head still throbbing). We claimed our beds, washed out clothes, and chatted to our friend Kath from New Zealand, and a new friend Patsy. We found out that Kath is an artist (She drew the pencil drawing at the beginning of this diary). It took a while, but my pain eventually subsided before bedtime, and I slept well.

Diary entry by Karen

Today we walked from Hornillos to Castrojeriz. It amazed us that we had walked the first 10km in two hours. We had walked half of the day's route by 8.30am, stopped for a cuppa and then kept walking. A lovely surprise greeted us when we got to San Anton, and we saw the ruins of a convent there, with a hospital for pilgrims, which is now an albergue. Within the ruins of the convent grounds is the most amazing place of peace, with cast iron tables and chairs, a lovely garden and a welcoming host.

Later, we bumped into Gary and Sue, as we headed to Castrojeriz, together, arriving by 12 noon. After the usual routine of showers, hand washing clothes and having a rest, we stayed in a fantastic municipal albergue run by two lovely chaps who are extremely accommodating.

Although we are in the Meseta, which is supposed to be mentally hard, we have had such a lovely walk today. The peace of the walk with no towns or city traffic was a pleasant change.

A lovely day, with the most gorgeous sunrise

THOUGHT of the day by Karen

Today we have spent the day walking along lovely earth tracks between fields and on the edge of a cliff. It was so peaceful, with no traffic and no noise of a town or city. The occasional road was a country road style with barely any traffic.

The thing that grabbed my attention today was the rhythm or music of nature. Being In a remote place meant we heard the wheat swaying in the gentle breeze and the birds singing their chorus. It was so magical.

It reminded me of Jesus' triumphant entry into Jerusalem and him saying, "I tell you, if these were silent, the very stones would cry out." Another lovely passage is, For you shall go out in joy and be led forth in peace; the mountains and the hills before you shall break forth into singing, and all the trees of the field shall clap their hands (Isaiah 55:12).

How often do we listen to nature praising God? Have a listen and see what you think.

Thank you, Lord, that when we are in a place of silence, we can hear creation singing praises to you. Amen

The ruins

Our Camino Diary - Day 16

The meseta

A water tap with a tao (The weird T-shaped cross).

OUR CAMINO DIARY - DAY 17
17TH MAY

Castrojeriz to Fromista. (24.9km)

DIARY ENTRY by Karen

Today has been a challenging day, a test of endurance. The weather was chilling wind. Regardless of the weather, you have to leave the hostel. So, with gloves, hats and raincoats, we went out into the cold. The day started with a 12% ascent up a hill (2952 ft according to the altimeter in Brett's watch) followed by an 18% descent on the other side.

After that we were on the Meseta with no shelter. We were hoping to only do 19.1km in those weather conditions, but the place we wanted to stay at looked like a ghost town. Brett, and I decided to go an extra 5.8km to Fromista, and we both arrived cold and extremely tired.

After seeing the weather on the TV a couple of days ago, we knew it wouldn't be so hot. But I did not expect the rain we had last night. Some houses in the town had flood defences in the doorways, so that should've been a giveaway.

It hammered it down with rain, and the house didn't even rattle. No shakes, no nothing.

DIARY ENTRY by Brett

We woke up this morning, made breakfast and gave a donation again. We left late and put on our wet weather gear, expecting rain. After a while, we came to a bridge with the following words etched into it.

Romanos 11:1-27

Thankfully, it didn't rain, but it was windy, a chilly wind. We walked along a long winding road to a hill. A 10% incline, and 18% decline, with a windbreak at the top.

The windbreak offered words of wisdom from other pilgrims. One wrote "it's easy to make it difficult for yourself ". After a much-needed sweet break, we walked down the hill to more stony path's and winding tracks. The rain had left big puddles, and we soon felt our boots heavy with mud, all the time the wind was at our side constantly freezing us. After what felt like hours, we arrived at the san Nicholas de Peuntelitero Hospital de Peregrinos.

Inside was a long table with an altar at the end. Pilgrims were sitting and enjoying a drink and a biscuit. We made a donation and bought a lemon and a stamp for the credential. We left and walked some more, and feeling tired, decided we would stay in Boadillo.

When we got there, we soon changed our mind and walked an extra mile with the icy wind still at our side. Boadillo was simply a ghost town, one albergue, and no bar, so nowhere to eat. As we approached Fromista, we walked alongside the canal with our Camino friends Sue and Gary from Australia. We reached the lock, took some photos and headed to our albergue.

We booked in and went to sleep straight away. The constant wind had completely wiped both of us out. Later, we bumped into Kath (New Zealand artist), and Patsy (UK). Karen and I went out to grab supplies for tomorrow and for a Pilgrims meal. First course salad (nice), second course microwave lasagna (yuck) third course cheesecake (very nice) and some Kas Limon of course.

Tomorrow? Not sure what's happening for now. We are going to sleep with the sound of guitar playing as some pilgrims celebrate a birthday.

THOUGHT of the day by Karen

Today is a day of small blessings. During the night it had rained, and this morning was extremely cold and windy. Usually the flat plains have no shade; which means today it had no wind break except the pilgrims.

So the small blessings

1. It didn't rain (yay)

2. I listened to some music on my MP3 that I hadn't heard for a long time. It was like having a praise party in my head.

3. We were able to stop to warm up and be refreshed

More pictures of the Meseta.

A small church with a donativo, where we stopped. Brett bought a lemon to put in his water.

424km to go before we finish (almost halfway).

OUR CAMINO DIARY - DAY 18
18TH MAY

Fromista to Carrión (19.3km).

Diary entry by Karen

Although it was a warmer day than yesterday, it wasn't by much. We did really well as walking went, as we were at Carrión before the albergue opened. It was a superb albergue, run by Argentinian nuns, all really young. It was explained to us; they were all novices and postulates. The young lady in charge had been a nun for sixteen years. The welcome was amazing, and they invited us to a musical evening

Diary entry by Brett

Breakfast was served at 6:30am. We ate sweetbreads with juice and coffee, then on towards Carrion at 19.3km (12m).

We spent most of the morning getting blown about again, but this time, we dodged in and out of coffee shops to keep warm with hot drinks and bathroom breaks.

After a while, we had a choice to make... go left and walk along the main road, or go right and take the extra half a kilometre down the pretty route along the river. Simple choice. We walked along the river together, and eventually ended up at our albergue in Carrión, run by some lovely nuns. As we inched into the albergue, we noticed an entire room full of backpacks in the centre, and a long queue of pilgrims sat around the outside edges of the room on benches. After paying for our beds and grabbing a stamp for our credentials, we were provided with a room. We went through the usual routine of claiming our beds, having a shower and sharing a washing machine with another pilgrim. We ate and went downstairs to see the nuns in the main reception room with guitars singing, and the place filled with pilgrims sat on benches, on the floor, and on the stairways.

One nun played guitar and spoke in Spanish, while another interpreted for her in English. They sang beautifully, and when it was over, they asked each pilgrim for their name, where they had come from, and the reason they were doing the Camino. Some reasons ranged from "I just fancied a walk" to " I am doing a sabbatical" to "I am here for a loved one". The entire experienced had really affected some people, and there were tears, and very heartfelt moments and stories.

After this, they invited us to a pilgrims' mass. We were each given a multicoloured paper star as a reminder that, even in the darkness, there is light. I stuck my star in my journal as a reminder of this day.

We spent the rest of the evening relaxing in the dining room area, chatting with a lady from Australia about what the plan is for tomorrow, and based on the fact that there are so few beds available at our destination.

THOUGHT of the day by Karen

Today has been a day of choosing to walk alongside the road or walk alongside a river. Both routes are parallel to each other and you can see others walking the other path. It reminded me of a YouTube video "life is like a cup of coffee".

It doesn't matter which path you take. They are both of equal value and they both go to the same place. It's personal preference. We are all on a journey of life and what makes the journey unique is us, because we are all different. What matters is being happy and content with the path we have chosen. As a person of faith, I love this quote, "to act justly, to love mercy and walk humbly with your God (Micah 6)".

Tonight, we shared two of the most beautiful acts of worship. We are staying at a convent and the 1st thing was a musical evening. We sang hymns in Spanish and English and everyone shared their name, where they were from and why they were doing the Camino. It was really moving because people were extremely honest and vulnerable. The second was mass, inside the church, attached to the convent. After the service, which was in Spanish, the priest asked all the pilgrims to go forward. He asked for a show of hands as he named countries and welcomed people. He said a prayer over everyone and then he and the nuns prayed a blessing over every pilgrim individually and gave us a star. It was a reminder that although we are all walking the Camino and united in all the trials and tribulations; we are all having a unique experience because God has something different for each one.

I wonder if you are enjoying and happy with your journey?

Scenic route through woodland.

One of the many storks' nests that are around the area.

Our Camino Diary - Day 18

A metal cutout of a pilgrim.

OUR CAMINO DIARY - DAY 19
19TH MAY

Carrión to Ledigos.

Post by Brett

Today is our 19th day on the Camino, and we are now well over the halfway mark.

Every single day has been full of unique experiences, and some sort of pain, either physical or mental.

Today's pain for me, was the fact that I lost my bank card... so I quickly froze it, and now I am glad that I took the advice (from the many tutorials, journals and videos before we came) about bringing two bank cards, yay :)

Today, we started our walk at 6:30am, and found a sign that told us it was 3 degrees centigrade.

After 25.8km of roughly the same sort of scenery (we've got this for 10 days) and only 2 water taps to fill up our bottles, we arrived at Ledigos - Terradillos de Templarios. The walk was pretty easygoing, reasonably flat all day, and mainly road, gravel pathways, and some rocky tracks. Eventually it became sunny, but we still had a chilly breeze.

We also bumped into some of our new Camino friends; a couple from Australia, an artist from New Zealand, (The lady who drew the picture at the front of this book), her friend from the UK and the lady from America. All these people and several more now seem to travel at roughly the same pace as we are.

Tomorrow we are off to somewhere else with a really long name, and another long chunk of mileage. I will post more details then.

THOUGHT of the day by Karen

Today is the second day of feeling that after a walk I could read something more than a novel. Each day until now I have felt drained and my brain is mush.

All this means we are getting used to this new routine. Our bodies are adjusting and suddenly we can cope with more. I've thought of what's next. Are there things I need to take with me to my new appointment? What do I need to read as forward planning and what questions do I have?

It's a reminder for me that all new things seem to take all our time at first and can feel overwhelming and then suddenly it all seems manageable. Let's see what the future holds.

What new things are you doing? Are you feeling overwhelmed? Can you see a light at the end of the tunnel?

SORRY, but there are no photos today.

OUR CAMINO DIARY - DAY 20
20TH MAY

Ledigos to Bercianos. (20.5km)

Diary entry by Karen

Today was a pleasant walk because it was warm. Leaving at 6 am , we had breakfast in the first town and a snack when we hit Sahagun. We didn't have a look around and no churches seemed to be open en route. We had trouble locating the Albergue because directions were rubbish and Brett maps had the wrong location. However, we got there early and had our backpacks once again in a queue.

We chose this hostel because it's a donativo offering a communal meal, pilgrim service, and breakfast. Today there was a period of time being disconcerted because the undergrowth on either side of us was moving. I didn't see any creatures, though. I thought about yesterday and today and, on reflection, I like the days where you are walking from one village to the next. It's shorter on the longer walks like yesterday 17 km without a town, toilets or water. I was like a little kid thinking, "are we there yet ?"

What this highlights to me is, that I need to break tasks down more at work and at home to keep me focused.

We have just had the most amazing night. This albergue is a donativo (donation-based) that offers a bed, evening reflections, an evening meal and breakfast. You pay what you think it is worth. The evening meal we all ate together, was paella in two big pans. We all had seconds, and some even had thirds. They got us all to sing a pilgrim song together and then, as hosts, they sang to us. They had worked out which countries were staying and they called each up one by one to sing a song from their country. It was brilliant and everyone joined in. We find that the evening prayers, the communal meals, and the evening laughter are brilliant for creating friendships. At the end of the meal, they said that women usually do all the work at home so... could 6 men do the washing up in the kitchen? I'm currently in bed while Brett and others are in the kitchen.

Another amazing experience

Post by Brett

Today is really exciting, but more about that later.

After the usual wake up, rolling up our sleeping bags, toilets, wrapping what items we had in bags, and clipping our shoes to the back of our bags, all while in pitch black, we set off at 6:30am (which seems to be our usual at the moment) and headed to where the yellow arrows took us.

Some walking later, on dusty roads and gravel footpaths, we bumped into the Australian couple who we were getting to know.

They walked with us, and even spent breakfast time with us, then afterwards, we walked some more. A while later, we found ourselves on our own again and heading towards our intended destination 23km away.

But.... before that, we spotted a stone bridge, and a church on the other side of it, and once again the yellow arrows pointed us that way. We couldn't go into the church as it was closed, however, we saw something which grabbed our attention.

On our left and right, as we walked along, were some strange-looking sculptures.

Further on were two tall statues facing each other, and on the bottom of the left statue were some words, which, when translated, said that we were now officially halfway along the Camino. We got really excited. Time for a photo opportunity, and by now our Australian friends had caught up again, and joined in the photo opportunity too.

Afterwards we carried along the trail of roads, and gravel and rocks, and eventually got to Bercianos, and walked all around several times to find the albergue, but with sat nav giving the wrong position, and part of the road freshly tarmacked and no yellow arrows, it took us quite a while.

We are currently in a donation based hostel and have claimed our beds, done our washing, and even had to hang the washing line we packed (just a length of para cord and some safety pins), as the other lines have run out of space. Our New Zealand Artist and her UK Camino friend are here, so is the man from Hungary (who we are glad is here, as we had heard that a man from Hungary had a heart attack) and so are the sisters from Ireland.

Tomorrow, not so far... I think.

THOUGHT of the day by Karen

1. Today I have been thinking about friendship. We had a

lovely evening with Kath and Patsy last night and this morning we walked with Gary and Sue. I have an amazing family who is extremely supportive and encouraging of one another, but we all need friends as well; friends that have the same hobbies, friends at work, friends who live in our area, friends who have a shared experience, friends walking the same journey. We are so thankful for the people we have met on the way and are sharing this experience with.

2. Today we walked between towns, so some stretches 3 km, some 6km, but each time a short distance from a town. In comparison, yesterday and tomorrow we had long stretches without knowing how far we have done and how far left. I find myself 'thinking as a child', asking 'are we there yet?' It has made me realise that at work and home I need to break tasks down smaller so that it doesn't seem so long before they are accomplished. I think that will help me not to procrastinate (don't laugh).

The left statue with engraving on the bottom which says we are halfway.

Our official Camino halfway Selfie !!

Our Camino Diary - Day 20 55

An evening with Kath from New Zealand, and her friend Patsy from the UK.

An inspirational message. "We are all broken, that's how the light gets in".

OUR CAMINO DIARY - DAY 21
21ST MAY

Bercianos to Mansilla de las Mullas

DIARY ENTRY by Brett

A short post today, I'm tired and need to sleep.

We got up, had a bit of a naff breakfast, walked 23k and then found our albergue... which does our washing for us, yay.

We also saw some lizards on the way :)

Tomorrow we head into the city of Leon, woohoo !!!

DIARY ENTRY by Karen

Today was an okay walk. There was a big bit of 13 km that seem to last forever. However, when we got to Mansilla, we booked into a lovely albergue which had a courtyard. The hostalero was lovely and extremely accommodating. We continued to bond as a group even though some will leave as the Camino calls them on.

Our Camino Diary - Day 21 57

Our breakfast, yes... that is tea, in a bowl!!

(View from a bridge) Most of the motorways are like this all day. I think we probably saw 10 cars, all day.

A quote from "The Way"(starring Martin Sheen and Emilio Estevez), or did "The Way" use the quote from the bridge? We may never know. It says "You don't choose a life, you live one".

OUR CAMINO DIARY - DAY 22
22ND MAY

Mansilla de las Mullas to Leon

POST BY BRETT

Today was a day of goodbyes. Goodbye to Mansilla, goodbye to our UK friend Patsy and our New Zealand friend Kath, goodbye to the two Irish sisters who are doing the Camino in separate portions over several years, and goodbye to our friend from the USA as well. As we walk to León and prepare to stay for two nights (with a break day in the middle), we learnt that some of our Camino friends will carry on. We wished them all a "Buen Camino", and will be happy to send them pictures of our arrival in Santiago, perhaps even bump into them again?

Today's walk was very quiet. We hardly saw any other pilgrims. Although we only did 18k, I was very slow, and limped most of the way, but hey, we got there at around 12pm and only had to wait for a few minutes for our hostel to open.

With backpacks in our room, we rested for a while before heading into town for a look round. We went to the museum (sorry photos not allowed) where they have on show, a chalice, that is claimed to be the holy grail, the goblet of Christ from the last supper.

The frescos (wall paintings) were simply breathtaking and definitely told lots of stories.

Then it was ice cream time.

After a short break, we headed back to the hostel to rest during the hottest part of the day (siesta) and then went out again for a look around and Karen had a mushroom pizza while I ate salami pizza (we also tried sangria, yummy).

The end of the day is fast approaching and we have now retired for the night, watching the Big Bang theory in Spanish lol

Until tomorrow ... hasta luego (see you later)

DIARY ENTRY by Karen

Today we had a great start. There were some novelty things to see, like the vending area with the pilgrim and signpost. We had a break after every 5 km, which works well for us. It was difficult for Brett today as we were walking into Leon (Foot trouble). At the entrance to Leon, there was a tourist information stand for pilgrims. We got our credential stamped, and a map of Leon with important things to see. We were asked where we were staying and they highlighted it on the map and then gave us a lolly each. It was such a good welcome. Today was also a sad day because we have said goodbye to both Kath (Our New Zealand Friend) and (her UK friend) Patsy. Patsy is taking the bus forward a couple of days because she is running out of time. Kath is not having a rest day like we are. It's amazing how people can touch you, even though we have only known them for a week. We went to the Museo San Lordono de Leon which has some 12th century frescoes which were really interesting. I would like to do some more reading about the museum. I had a guided tour in Spanish because the English version wasn't until Friday and that's when we walk again. We have had a lovely ice cream in the evening air and have gone back to our room for a rest before going out this evening.

THOUGHT of the day by Karen

Today I have had lots of thoughts. It was a brief journey but so much to make an impression.

1. Today has been a day of saying goodbye to some friends who have travelled with us this last week. We hugged Patsy, Kath and the Irish ladies as they continue their journeys forward. Although some people we have known since the beginning and others for a short time, we have journeyed together and shared joys and sorrows and aching feet lol . We have all made an impression on each other and contributed to each other's journeys. Even though we do not journey forward together, we wish them Buen Camino and pray that God will continue to guide them on their pilgrimage.

2. The welcome we received on entering Leon overwhelmed us. There was a free information point for pilgrims that was manned with some lovely gents. They offered us maps, asked where we were staying and wrote on the map to highlight where our albergue was, stamped our credentials and gave us a lolly. It made me think about 'what

kind of welcome do we give to others coming to visit, or work or church?' If we were more welcoming, would that make people feel more welcome? Is there a point where it's too much? It's worth a ponder.

Pizza and Sangria

The welcome booth, with maps, stamps, and lollies.

We had an amazing welcome as we got to León

León Cathedral

OUR CAMINO DIARY - DAY 23
23RD MAY

Rest Day in León

POST BY BRETT

So, today we had a rest day in León and boy, did we need it.

The pollen count is through the roof and everyone is sneezing. It completely covered the streets in white fluff, but it's still not as bad as yesterday when the inside of the bar we ate tea at looked like it had a white furry carpet (all the doors are open because of the heat, and the wind just blows the pollen in).

We got up at about 10ish today, went downstairs out of our double room into León.

Breakfast was croissants and earl grey tea with some tapas (small tasters of a chocolate style food which was tasty) and we then headed out to the cathedral. The weather was quite downcast, and it looked like it would chuck it down with rain and while we were inside the cathedral it soon changed and became very hot indeed.

We had a little walk to the pilgrims' plaza and took some pictures.

In Spain, because the sun becomes so hot, their morning, noon and evening are different. The morning is from approx 8am to 2pm, and by then it is too hot to work, so schools send children home, workers go home and everyone has siesta (sleep), and the entire place becomes a ghost town, until approx 7pm when all the businesses open again including the kitchens. This gives everyone the chance to eat tea at night-time before bed. If we adopted this in the western world, we would probably enjoy life more, instead of constantly complaining about the heat during Summer.

So, we have siesta'd and now; we are just chilling in our room, waiting for shops to open.

Diary entry by Karen

Today we have enjoyed the little luxuries of getting up late, enjoying a fabulous breakfast, and no walking (yay). We have looked around the cathedral that is beautiful in its simplicity. It's made in Gothic style with loads of stain glass windows. We learnt it is east facing because that's where the Sun rises. The stained glass depicts the life of Christ behind the altar. Where there is the most light to its right, where the Sun will travel during the morning, because all the apostles knew the light, and spread the word. To its left, but never gets the Sun, are the Old Testament prophets that never knew the light, but were faithful followers. The entire front was made to help people feel as close to heaven as possible.

We walked to San Marcos Plaza and took pictures next to the pilgrim.

. . .

THOUGHT of the day by Karen

Today we went to have a look around Leon Cathedral. It was so beautiful and simplistic. I was really taken with the stained glass windows.

They built the Cathedral in Gothic style to carry the faithful to a completely different world to the one that exists outside, creating a transcendent atmosphere of colour and spirituality.

The main central glass behind the altar is the life of Christ. This gets the sun as it rises and for the rest of the day. To the right of this, the glass shows the apostles. As the sun moves during the morning, the light gradually shines through these panes. They knew Jesus as the light of the world and told others about the light. To the left are the Old Testament prophets in glass. These panes never get the sun. The Old Testament prophets never knew the light, but they were faithful to God and hoped for the light.

How amazing is it that so much thought went into a building at the moment of design to create such beauty and spiritual meaning? I wonder how many prayers and chants were sung and heard during this period of history, before the renaissance came and changed everything.

I wonder how we can use light to help carry people to a different place than the world outside, to connect with God, if only for a moment.

The bronze statue of a pilgrim at the pilgrims plaza.

3 Dimensional bronzed amp of León

Some windows inside the cathedral.

OUR CAMINO DIARY - DAY 24
24TH MAY

Leon to Mazariffe.

Post by Brett

Last night we hardly got any sleep. The nightlife in Leon went on until 2am with stragglers singing drunkenly until about 4 in the morning, and me being sick with suspected food poisoning.

We got up, got dressed and left the hostel and went out into the street, where we uncovered Spain's secret. We always wondered how Spain was always so clean, and now we understand why. The street cleaners are up early with hosepipes, washing away the rubbish and washing the streets clean. So, Spain does get dirty !!!

Anyway, we spent about two hours walking out of the city and then decided... pretty route or road?... pretty route it was.

For a "pretty route" we seemed to spend a fair amount of time walking along a small road (but hey, it's better than the main highway with its rush hour traffic of 5 cars an hour), and we only saw the odd car or two.

Later on, we were kicking up the dust again on the dirt track path and came across more wine cellars that looked a bit like hobbit holes, as we approached our destination Villar de Mazarife.

We spotted the albergue (hostel) and were quite surprised at some of the quirkiness of various things here. They have a concrete pool with ladder, which is painted blue inside and walls which are raised above the ground (basically a large concrete-walled trough, in the garden with no lid, and no water).

There is a built-in bar, which looks like it is full of locals, and the pilgrims' eating area, which is full of pilgrims we don't recognise. In fact, I don't think we have seen a single pilgrim we recognise today.

The best bit is, we have a room for ourselves, for 14 euros total, with our own electric sockets (woohoo) our own light (so no one can wake us up in the morning). Also, and this is the best bit, we have our own door!!!

This is of major importance because... in Spain, the government charges the hostels extra tax per room, so the hostel owners remove all the internal doors to keep their taxes down.

Side note: we watched on tv yesterday that someone was arrested, for turning his garage into a hostel for 150 people.... apparently that's illegal here.

So, we've done our washing, it's on the line and we are just chilling, as we enjoy siesta and wait for our clothes to dry.

Tomorrow? Astorga- 30k - will we make it, or will we wimp out and go to the stop before it?

. . .

DIARY ENTRY by Karen

Today started off a boring day, especially considering the first 9 km was a roadside around the city. As soon as we change to the alternative path, everything changed. For a while, it felt like walking down a country lane and then it changed to some tracks with the most amazing views. All in one view, we could see mountains capped with snow, trees and fields.

You could hear crickets, locusts, and frogs. It was an amazing walk in God's garden. Listening to Christian music it was a perfect day. Brett really struggled, though. We think he had a dose of food poisoning the day before, so wasn't his normal self.

Went into a church here that is dedicated to Saint James. I took some pictures of the stories.

THOUGHT of the day by Karen

We took the alternative route today, to get away from the highway and have the scenic route. It was amazing. For parts, it was like walking down a country lane and for others we were walking on a sandy path. The scenery was beautiful. All in one scene you had snow-capped mountains in the background and then trees and fields. You could hear nature all around; crickets, locusts, frogs and birds. It was such a lovely walk. Compared to the city of Leon yesterday, it was peaceful and a solitude walk. For large amounts of time, it felt like we were the only people on the road.

It was a lovely walk in God's garden. When was the last time you went for a solitary walk in a peaceful place and admired God's garden?

Our Camino Diary - Day 24 73

Wine cellar or hobbit hole?

A pilgrim cutout

Our very own room !!! (We even have a key)

OUR CAMINO DIARY - DAY 25
24TH MAY

Mazariffe to Astorga. (32km)

Diary entry by Brett

Today was probably our hardest day yet.

The mileage (32k = 20m) wasn't really a problem. Our key problems were my ankle, Karen's foot and the heat. 24 degrees. (nearly 80 degrees F, with a 12lb backpack, and walking.

We headed out at 6:23am, and after a while, found ourselves on another tarmac road. With beautiful sunrises in the background, we soon reached more stone roads. Very difficult to walk on. We went ahead and eventually found shade in the trees, but also found lots of pollen. More rocky pathways later and we reached a place to have breakfast, some croissants and tea. Carrying on along the trail, we came across a town where we saw walls built like cobbled pavements. After some bridges and a bit of road walking, we came across some storks nesting on a mobile phone tower. Later we came across a place where the locals were setting up for some mediaeval jousting in a tournament next month. It looked very grand. We stopped by for a kas limon (a bitter lemon soft drink) and bocadillas (baguettes). The portions were small and expensive and the hotel owner didn't seem to get involved with pilgrims at all.

We carried on and after more villages arrived in Astorga. We got a room (right at the top (more stairs)) and met a lady from Italy called Jade (pronounced Jarda) and a guy from Czech republic called Patrick.

After resting and showers, we went out for tea. The experience inside the bar was a bit of a surprise. After waiting for 20 minutes to be noticed, we were told to go outside, as the inside was only for locals.

We soon changed venues and were glad we did because we had the best dining experience. First course-salad, second course- soul and chips, third course-ice cream and red wine for €11.

Sorry, no photos today, as it was late, and we were exhausted. Tomorrow, we are off to Rabanal.

Diary entry by Karen

Today was a hard day. Even though we left early, it took us till 5 pm to reach Astorga. Brett found today really hard with his ankle. I kept encouraging him during the day, gave options to stop, but he was determined. By the time we got there, we were both exhausted. We showered, rested, and went out for some tea. It was an accomplishment we both completed today, but we were both worse for wear.

Sorry, no pictures today, as the scenery is pretty much the same, just long dusty trail across the Meseta with no shade.

OUR CAMINO DIARY - DAY 26
26TH MAY

Astorga to Rabanal (20km)

POST BY BRETT

Wow, I woke up to the sound of clattering - Karen (on top bunk) must have rolled over to switch her mobile phone alarm off and inadvertently her mobile usb battery pack and kindle slid from the top bunk through the gaps and gravity sent them hurtling towards my head on the bottom bunk. It was very loud (clanging on the metal bars) and rather scary. I will change ends, so that if it rains electronics again, they hit my feet, not my head (which thankfully didn't happen today). I'm just pleased it was me on the bottom bunk, not some other unsuspecting pilgrim, that could have been interesting.

We got up, got dressed, got packed, and got out.

It wasn't too long before we were eating breakfast.... two pieces of ham and toast and 2 teas for €11:20, the most expensive breakfast so far, and it didn't even taste that good.

We left Astorga and picked up the pace a bit. My left

ankle was now very swollen indeed for all the twisting. Since I can't take ibuprofen tablets with the meds I am on, I relied on my adrenalin instead.

Before long, we got to a small church (not open) and spotted the pilgrims' prayer (for the Cruz de Ferro tomorrow) on the outside porch. We took some photos and carried on. More highlights of our way included:

- a cowboys bar
- more storks' nests on church chimneys
- a man dressed as a knight helping a children's charity. I held his hawk and even stroked it for a while. Karen took some pics, and then a couple more pics of me with the knight.
- More rocky uphill pathways
- the fence with a mile of crosses in it. Karen and I made a cross and said a prayer for all pilgrims.

We then got to our albergue, and the owner told us that the massage person was not working because today was a Sunday, also the pharmacy was closed. He asked about my legs and I told him about my swollen ankle, and he instantly gave me a free ankle support. We had lunch, Karen did the washing while I soaked my ankle, then our Australian friends who we got reunited with chatted to us in the garden while I elevated my ankle to reduce the swelling.

We ate tea and then went to find a church with Gregorian singers we had heard about, and listened to them singing. After that we both went back to the albergue to write the journals and blog, and now.... sleep time, tomorrow is another long day.

Diary entry by Karen

Today we started really strong. Brett got into the adrenaline zone and was off, sometimes much faster than me. That waned after a time. There were some great stops today for drinks and we took full advantage of that.

Today we came to the fence of crosses, which was hard to walk past and not just because of the terrain. Each cross represents people's loss, grief, faith, hopes. It's a special light place that lasts about 1 km.

Just before that, we came to a man raising money for a children's charity. Brett had a picture taken with him and his bird of prey. He encouraged us to go tonight to vespers at the church of Rabanal. Vespers was a Gregorian chant with some monks. It was a hard service to follow, but also exquisite.

Brett has received some help today for his foot. With the pharmacy and massage parlour, both being closed because it is a Sunday, the hostalero gave Brett an ankle support and others advised his legs being raised and placing in cold water. Thankfully tonight his foot is doing much better.

I'm not sure we are going to manage all the stages of the next few days, but we are going to go as far as we can and then stop. We are learning to be wise and not let others influence us.

Thought of the day by Karen

Today as we were coming into Rabanal de Camino there is about 1km of crosses that people have made and placed on the wire fence. It was a little eerie to walk past at first, and then it became slightly difficult and not just the terrain (which were stones on a slope that looked ploughed). Each cross represented a pilgrims: grief, loss, faith and hope.

Pilgrims would have made a cross for many reasons and placed it there.

I made a cross, and as I was doing so, I was thinking about my life. I decided a long time ago to become a Christian and I have accepted my calling. All I need to do now is to carry my cross and live life, which is the hard bit. It's not always easy to say you're a Christian and to live by it. It's something to work on every day.

I wonder, how you are doing at carrying your cross?

Our cross with the green grass around the middle.

Our Camino Diary - Day 26

A man was raising money for a children's charity and was allowing people to take a picture with his bird of prey for a donation.

The cowboy bar

The knight let me hold his sword. It was a lot heavier than I had expected, and I have no idea how he could wear chainmail in the middle of the day. It was so hot.

OUR CAMINO DIARY - DAY 27
27TH MAY

Rabanal to El Acebo (16.5km)

DIARY ENTRY by Brett

Today we reached the Cruz De Ferro. This was an important part of the Camino for me, as I had carried a small stone with me from our garden to lie at the foot of the cross. Each pilgrims' stone represents something personal in their life. Grief, losing a loved one, or some trials throughout their life. I pulled out a pen and wrote on my stone. 'Rest in Peace Dad, love you lots Brett x'. Since the loss of my father in 2012, and my epilepsy making it impossible to attend his funeral hundreds of miles from where I lived at the time, I have found it difficult to let go, and this was my chance to say goodbye, in the same country he died in. Thankyou dad for always believing in me, loving me, and helping me grow into the person I am today. Love you always Brett x

. . .

DIARY ENTRY by Karen

Today has been a challenging day. Over the past weeks, Brett has hurt his knee, and he has a knee brace. About a week ago, he hurt his ankle by twisting it over rocks. Yesterday he had to soak his feet and elevate to make the swelling go down. A kind hostalero gave him an ankle support which has really helped today. Today was 19km over rocky stones with pretty much no reprieve. We decided today, not to walk as far as the guidebook suggested. Today was supposed to be 25km, tomorrow 31km, and day after 28.5km. We knew we couldn't do three long days, so we are hoping to split them into 4 days instead.

We reached the Iron Cross today, Cruz de Ferro, and placed our stones on the mound. We then continued up another mountain path to the highest point on the Camino. The views today have been amazing, enhanced by the wild flowers on each side of the path and their smell. We arrived in El Acebo at 1.30pm, had lunch and came to a hostel that is a donativo. They provided a communal meal tonight, a bed, and breakfast in the morning.

We are now resting and writing our journals

DIARY ENTRY by Karen

Today we left early, knowing that it was going to be quite a climb. Unfortunately, most of the way was over Rocky stones. This meant that we went slowly. Brett had already hurt his ankle and knee, so we needed to go at a sensible pace. Brett and I then stopped for breakfast in the only town, which was great. We had already decided that we wouldn't manage the length of the next three days and, therefore; we were going to create our own stages. The most important thing is finishing the Camino, not the time in which you do it. The walk today went past Cruce de Ferro, which was fantastic.

It was an opportunity to leave a stone behind. Mine represented everything negative that happened in ministry. I want to go into my new stationing as a confident me, not weighed down by other people's versions of ministry.

We have stopped at El Acebo and have gone to a donativo hostel. The hostaleros are extremely welcoming and have made people feel at home. We are having a relaxing afternoon after showering, washing clothes et cetera. This donativo offers an evening meal as well, which will be really nice as a community.

THOUGHT of the day by Karen

Today we reached Cruce de Ferro, where we placed our stones. Pilgrims are encouraged to bring a stone from home, carry it as part of the pilgrimage and place it on the mound of the iron cross. People do this for two reasons; to ask forgiveness for a sin they have committed, or as a symbol of leaving something behind and therefore your pack being lighter afterwards.

Each one of us picks up baggage as we travel through life; fears, anxieties, regrets, the opinions of others etc... and it's good to think about what we don't need to carry anymore. Things we can leave behind and go into the future with confidence.

What are the things you need to put down today to enable you to walk into your future?

The road to the Cruz de Ferro (The Iron Cross).

The Cruz de Ferro. On top of this mound of stones and wooden pole is an iron cross. The mound of stones is made up of thousands of rocks which pilgrims bring, to say goodbye to a loved one, or let go of some trouble in their life.

A moment in prayer, as I said goodbye to my father (who died in Spain), and left my stone at the foot of the Cruz de Ferro with my father's name written on it. This is the main reason I came on this pilgrimage. Karen left her stone too.

Sunset at the foot of the cross, close to our albergue in El Acebo

OUR CAMINO DIARY - DAY 28
28TH MAY

El Acebo to Ponferrata (16km).

Post by Brett

Today was reasonably easy on mileage, as my left ankle couldn't handle much more than the distance we walked.

We started off with breakfast (tea and toast), then grabbed our stuff and headed off down the road.

It wasn't too long before I realised I had left my coke bottle (filled with water) and carabiner back at the albergue, and instantly got to work on building another pilgrims' bottle holder (a simple bottle holder I fashioned from some para cord and a carabiner).

Several kilometres of tarmac, then dirt track, through another ghost town, up lots of mountain rock paths, with awkward blades and gulleys, and then down the same sort of thing. Walking along, one pilgrim we met last night recognised us and had actually picked up my bottle, and brought it along, hoping he would bump into me.... all was sorted. We ended up on dirt tracks with trees and bushes on either side, sometimes so close we had to squeeze ourselves through them. Then a road with a sign that looked very dangerous, like a car could slide off the edge of the road.

After that, a couple of miles of zig- zagging road like the sort of thing you might see in a suped-up car movie. We walked on the road, snaking down the mountain, with some parts of the cliff face so eroded that they had taken the safety barriers with them. Fortunately, someone had nailed some traffic cones to the side of the road as a temporary barrier.

At the end of the road, we approached a village and dropped into a bar for a drink and some food, and then off to the next place.

We finally arrived at Ponferrada, claimed bunks, and went for more food.

Later we came back, and met our room-mates from Poland, and found out that the man was a priest and would run tonight's pilgrims' mass.

After a good rest, we headed to the chapel on the grounds of the Albergue and observed mass. The service was mostly in Polish, but the bits in English talked about pilgrims, 'smelly on the outside, and changed / changing on the inside'.

After that, we headed into town and had a pizza.... the man in the pizza restaurant was the only staff, and he literally did everything... make the pizzas, cook, wash up, serve drinks, and lots more.

Tomorrow, we will see what happens. We may go further because I have an ankle support, some ibuprofen gel and 650mg paracetamol (the smallest I could get). They wanted to sell me 1 gram tablets, but I said no, lol.

. . .

DIARY ENTRY by Karen

We have taken things easy for a couple of days because of Brett and co-. So today we walked 16 km. Most of the day was okay underfoot, but there have been some enormous stones again that are not good for Brett.

We saw some amazing views while coming down the mountain. We had breakfast at a lovely hotel before walking home. The city here seems to be picturesque but we haven't explored yet. It has the only Castle on the Camino.

We have gone to a pharmacy and got Brett an ankle brace, ibuprofen gel and some very strong paracetamol we're hoping that he will feel better soon. We went to a Pilgrims mass which was taken by a fellow pilgrim who is a catholic priest. It was amazing. Although he said Mass in Polish, he gave prompts in English and a homily. The bible passage was from acts where Paul is in prison and there is an earthquake. He talked about all of us being pilgrims and how each day is new and different.

Through the experiences of each day, we are all being transformed by the holy spirit if we open up our hearts. This is a man who is obviously spirit filled, radiates the love of God and he is very much in love with Jesus, by the way the love shines through his eyes and his smiles when he presents the bread and wine. He is an inspiration from one priest to a minister. He has made me think about my faith and asked, "Do I radiate like that when I talk about Jesus and lead people in Holy Communion?". Another good day on the Camino.

THOUGHT of the day by Karen

We are in another donativo tonight, an albergue that accepts donations. This one is really modern with all facilities. They don't provide food, but they have a functional kitchen. As part of the albergue, they offer pilgrims' mass and a blessing. We went to the mass, and the priest is a fellow pilgrim and also the man we are sharing a 4 person dorm with.

It was the most spiritual and worshipful service of this Camino. He is a polish Catholic priest and therefore said the mass in polish. His English is very good even though he says it isn't, so he gave us prompts in English and did a homily in English about being a pilgrim and how the experience will transform us all. He glowed as a Christian and the reverence and the smile he gave when holding up the bread and wine was brilliant to see. It was truly inspiring and I would like to serve God in that way.

I wonder how the love of God and our love of Jesus radiates through us to others, so they can see God and worship him?

Caution - Low flying reindeer? Is that a Jet Engine? haha

Traffic cone safety barrier next to a sheer drop cliff. I would not want to drive this road at night-time.

Mountain stone pathways are really dangerous. It's easy to slip and do yourself damage on these.

OUR CAMINO DIARY - DAY 29
29TH MAY

Ponferrata to Villa Franca (25.3km)

DIARY ENTRY by Brett

Today started differently. Karen woke up and went to the bathroom while I opened my rucksack and hurriedly filled in the birthday card I had carried all the way from home. Then, when she came back, I gave her the card, and a small gift (a small Camino stone with an arrow pointing the way).

We left and headed towards the castle, then walked into the park, past the river, and across the bridge. The route then took us through the local neighbourhood and past a couple of statues, then onto a gravel path. We saw a building that shouldn't even stand, but through the best engineering I've seen, it does.

Afterwards, the signs with hands showed us the way towards our destination. We popped into a church and walked through vineyards which were soaking up the sun (at 28C / 82F) and by the time we had run out of water, we could see the town we were heading for.

After claiming bunks in our albergue, we met some people, and headed for the showers, and I rang one of my sons to wish him a happy birthday. After a well-deserved rest, we left the albergue and had a gentle stroll into town, helping a pilgrim who could not get into his hotel, and then on towards the town square. Karen's birthday meal was lovely. She had a chicken paella and a sangria. Today's journey may have been long at 25.3km, but it was flat, so relatively easy-going. Tomorrow, only the Camino knows what will happen.

DIARY ENTRY by Karen

This morning was a pleasant walk. We came to a park and down the road. The terrain was mostly nice to walk on and considering Brett's injuries; we made great time. We had a lovely lunch at Cacabelos; we noticed bacon bocadillos (baguette) for the first time and order two; they were delicious.

The last 8 km was slightly more difficult because most of it was through vineyards on farm tracks, which isn't so great for Brett.

Brett made me smile this morning with a surprise birthday card which he had travelled with from home and a lovely little Camino ornament to remember the trip with. It will make a significant addition to the prayer table.

THOUGHT of the day by Karen

Today I have been thinking about things that make me smile. Do you know it takes more effort and muscles to frown than it does to smile and it creates wrinkles too?

Smiles can be infectious. People can't help but like a smile even if they try not to.

The things that made me smile today were:

1. A birthday card Brett has been carrying for the past month and a small present as a souvenir of our journey.

2. Flowerpots made to look like flowerpot people.

3. We walked past a posh house that was alarmed to the hilt, but had these old people statues that are quite quirky

4. A pilgrim signpost outside a launderette, pointing the way

What makes you smile, and I wonder how many people you can make smile in a day by smiling at them?

The building that should fall over but doesn't.

Our Camino Diary - Day 29

A helping hand to show us the way.

"This way? Thanks pilgrim. Buen Camino"

OUR CAMINO DIARY - DAY 30
30TH MAY

Villa Franca to Ruitelan (19km)

Diary entry by Brett

There's not much to say about today's journey except... there were three routes. One route goes over the mountain, another less rigorous route and the third, the original Camino route which was pretty flat all the way. This route took us mostly on the footpath with the river on our left through the trees and to our right, and a road with a protective barrier to keep pilgrims safe.

We arrived at Ruitelan and got into our albergue called the pequenopotal, a cute little albergue for five euros for the bed, with the host, who is called Luis. We have been told that our tea later will be spaghetti carbonara, and Karen has told me she will eat it. I know she's not keen, but she seems to be trying out many experiences and really enjoying them.

Diary entry by Karen

The walk was mostly on roads and easy-going. The scenery wasn't overly fantastic, but I think our mood was swayed from the night before. We had the worst night's sleep of the whole Camino. We stopped because the next stage goes over a mountain and we were too tired to tackle it. The good news is when we stopped Brett's foot was not massive. It almost looked the same as the other one, so hopefully the ibuprofen gel is working.

We are at an Albergue that offers an evening meal and breakfast, so we don't need to go far. We have had lunch and crashed for most of the afternoon. Hopefully, we will be ready to tackle the mountain tomorrow.

Flowerpot friends.

We had been told that the scenery would not be "that interesting" then we saw this. The views were incredible.

Inside the bar where we had breakfast, people place money all over the stone-clad walls, anything from one cent coins to one euro.

OUR CAMINO DIARY - DAY 31
31ST MAY

Ruitelan to Hospital. (Hospital is the name of a village, not a building). 15km

Diary entry by Brett

Last night's albergue was probably our best experience. We went for tea at 19.30. We all gathered as pilgrims. On the long table were place settings, wine, water, and bread. The owner placed a bowl of creamy carrot soup on the table and asked one pilgrim to serve. After that we were told to help ourselves to salad. All the time the cook was having banter with us and taking the micky out of the Korean ladies, who were getting very flushed cheeks. We were then served the carbonara. As he went down the table, the cook took the plate off the last man and gave him the big serving bowl to eat out of. It was such an amazing night. We all bonded, even though we were all new. We were woken this morning to loud music.
- Ave Maria
- What a wonderful world

- Dance of the sugarplum fairy
- Feeling good
- Always look on the bright side of life

Everyone went to breakfast happily, thanked the hosts and left for the next leg of the journey.

One of my favourite things about today was a rock I found with the following words on it.

"Walking on earth is a miracle? What about walking on Earth?"

We visited a church where St. Francis of Assisi had visited and found a place that looked like it was in the medieval times called O'Cebreiro. Some tourists asked to have a picture with me 'a real live pilgrim!!!'

DIARY ENTRY by Karen

Today we are climbing up the mountain and down the other side. We had been led to believe that it was a really tough climb, but we found it ok. The up was some large stones in places, but in others, it was gravel paths. We stopped a few times because it was a really hot day and we needed drinks. We had some amazing chocolate cake and juice at Laguna de Castillo.

We had an interesting experience going into O'Cebreiro because it looked like a medieval hamlet with shops etc.. the commercial side of the Camino begins. There was a busload of tourists who wanted pictures of pilgrims, which was strange, but Brett was obliging. Then we stopped at a small hamlet called Hospital because it was getting too hot. We walked 15km today, crossing regions we are now in Galicia. We should come into Sarria in the next couple of days, which is the starting point if you want to receive a Compostela (certificate of completion of the Camino).

A lot of new pilgrims will arrive, for what some term as the "Disneyland Camino".

We thought that the Albergue hostaleros were not interested in the pilgrims because it was a government run hostel. We are going to try other types of hostel if we can.

THOUGHT of the day by Karen

Casa dos Pedrouzos

Today I've been thinking about all the pilgrims who have gone before us.

In the church in O'Cebreiro, there is a wall plaque that has come from Assisi as a tribute to Francis of Assisi doing the Camino in 1214. The conditions in his time would have been totally different to ours. Probably much harder conditions and less kept paths and roads. Water and food might have been more scarce, but a lot more hospitals (hostels) than today. Our experience is a little more comfortable. There are coffee shops etc on most days every 5km, and some roads and paths have been made better for pilgrims and a couple of re-routes because of the sheer volume of walkers. I think our experiences would be comparable. Even though the conditions are hard for us, the conditions that we live in are better. The challenges and hardships of the two different pilgrims are probably the same. Both pilgrims, even though years apart, are looking for a spiritual connection, to find that inner place that they might have lost or want to know more.

It's amazing to think that we have walked in the same pathways and from the same towns with such pilgrims as St. Francis of Assisi.

Lord, may we continue to follow the distinguished men and women of faith to draw closer to you. Amen

A small village called O'Cebreiro. Everyone here dresses up like Knights and Maids. It's very popular with tourists.

This stone sign says that we are now in Galicia

Plaque donated to commemorate St. Francis of Assisi

OUR CAMINO DIARY - DAY 32
1ST JUNE

Hospital to Triacastela.

Diary entry by Brett

Today we started earlier, to beat the heat. Leaving at 6am, we headed off into the dark with hat torches on, and saw the sun rise over the mountains. After a sharp incline and ascent to the top of the hill on gravel paths, we stopped for a cup of tea and something to eat. We met a big soppy dog (it was huge) from the albergue and he allowed me to stroke him.

Back on the road again, we plodded through farming villages with cows, machinery, that lovely smell of cowpat, and the millions of flies that come with it, but which you don't see until you disturb them by walking past. So, with my buff up, to avoid eating any "poo flies," we carried on through the wooded area. We walked past (in the middle of nowhere) a pharmacy dispensing machine... like a drinks dispenser with bandages and creams.

A little further, we arrived at stop number two, and the

climb uphill had made us hungry, so we cooled down with some more Kas Limon.

More track-walking later, we had a small stream on our left, the pathway in the centre, and a sheer drop to our right with beautiful views all around.

Another stop for some apple pie and a cup of tea, and we had enough energy to carry on to our last stop... Triacastela.

The albergue has lots of character, almost church-like, with its uneven wooden floors, beautiful beams, and antique vestry robes hung on the walls, which had been donated to the owner in the 80s.

The dining room table was made from old wooden doors, with the locks and handles still in place.

After claiming our bunks, we went shopping in the supermarket / grocers / tourist shop next door, and then went back to the albergue for some home-made / supermarket bought lunch of crusty rolls, butter portions and York ham and a cold drink.

The hostalero (host of the albergue) gave me a foot massage, and we spoke about his experiences in the Camino, and ours.

Later, we are off to the bar down the street to have some tea, but for now, we are just resting out of the heat of the sun.

Diary entry by Karen

Today was an easier day, even though Brett struggled towards the end. We had three stops along the way and arrived early, but in need of a rest. Todays albergue is private which means the owner cares about the pilgrims. He has given several people a foot massage, including Brett. We have had a supermarket next door and a pleasant group of pilgrims. This albergue is small, which adds to the charm.

THOUGHT of the day by Karen
Casa dos Pedrouzos

The kindnesses of others has been amazing today. A few people as they walked past us offered Brett meds today, because they could see he was having difficulty. When we arrived at the albergue, 3 Korean ladies offered us some food they had cooked and the hostalero was offering foot massages and had a look at Brett's foot. All these things have made our day a better day today.

I wonder if we realise how much impact our small kindnesses have on others? Or how our small kindnesses are small glimpses of heaven on earth.

Brett and I have been fans of the 'pay it forward' movement for quite some time. If you've not heard of it, give it a google.

This morning's sunrise

Our Camino Diary - Day 32

A pharmacy dispenser. You you can buy bandages, and blister plasters.

The dining table made from a reused door, and there were priests robes hung on the walls.

OUR CAMINO DIARY - DAY 33
2ND JUNE

Triacastela to Sarria.

Diary entry by Brett

We left the albergue and headed off into the darkness once again, to be greeted by one of Spains' stunning sunrises.

Walking through the countryside, we soon realised that this morning's walk was not for the faint-hearted. With steep climbs, heavy descents, and not much in the way of stops for almost the first 12k, we knew it was going to be tough, but we plodded on relentlessly.

As well as the pitch of the path changing constantly, the material we trod on changed very regularly. From flagstone paved roads, to gravel tracks, Rocky Mountain paths and wooded cuttings.

Eventually we came to the largest shell on the Camino so far, and a chance to rest for a few minutes. Next we got to a small place called Sanxil, and some smooth tarmac, easier for us both to walk on.

A quick change of scenery and walking through the woods, with more rocky paths, and even a fresh water stop, designed to look like a waterfall, with water collecting down the side of the track into a small stream.

We carried on through more old- looking villages and more uphill walking.

Exhausted, hot and hungry, we looked for a place to eat our supermarket supplies, and were completely surprised when we came across an oasis, or paradise garden. With tables of apples, banana, muesli, peaches, cherries and even hot coffee, we relaxed in this pilgrims' rest and rested our feet.

After an easy 20 minutes, we had finished our rocket fuel coffee, and homemade cake, then grabbed our packs, had a quick look around the inspirational quotes, leather chairs, wooden benches, and bookshelf, all outside, and absolutely buzzing with pilgrims. A couple have opened up their barn and yard as a donativo to pilgrims. It was a lavish spread and also were making coffee in the house. They encouraged pilgrims to paint, etc.. There were many inspirational quotes around.

This experience made me think of 2 things:

1) How can I be more generous and self-giving?

2) I want to start to collect quotes.

The atmosphere was so relaxing, it even contained a hugging zone.

After another hour, we stopped for another drink, and headed off again towards the town of Sarria, and the last 100km of the Camino. Unfortunately for Karen, this was not a nice piece of track, and as we passed the trees into town, she got bitten approximately 15 times within an hour.

We finished our walk with a trek across the town

towards our hostel for the next two nights and a rest day in Sarria.

Diary entry by Karen

It was a warm day, and the hill was much deeper than we thought. After 10 km we decided that rest day was probably in order so we booked a hostel for two nights. We are not sure how, but I have several bites all over my arms and back. We have checked my sleeping bag and stuff and it's not bedbugs.

Brett thought he saw a flea on me and brushed it off. Since getting into Sarria and out of the woods, I have changed my clothes and haven't been bitten again. My arm is really sore though which will hopefully wear off.

This stone says "The Important is to put great love in the small things - Mother Theresa"

Wise words "A Traveller is a human being on a spiritual journey, a pilgrim is a spiritual being on a human journey".

The Camino Shell. It's difficult to see in this photo, but this shell was easily the same height as we are. If you look closely, you can see Karen on the left.

OUR CAMINO DIARY - DAY 34
3RD JUNE

Rest Day - Sarria.

DIARY ENTRY by Brett

After a stiflingly hot night, I worked out that the blinds have a hidden vent in them, and around 2am the room cooled down enough for us to get some sleep.

Today, we had breakfast at the "Sleeping Sarria hostel" (which is more like a hotel), and met some of the other guests. We then retired to our room, and Karen and I spent most of the day just laying on the bed, watching tv, and resting.

We ate a supermarket lunch and later; watched the Spider-Man homecoming on Netflix, then went into town for the evening meal.

We have booked our flight and transport home today, so it's now etched in stone.

Patsy, (one of our Camino friends) has been in touch, to let us know she has now arrived in Santiago :), and I rang one of my sons to wish him a happy birthday.

Tomorrow, we are aiming for Portomarin (approx 22k) and may get wet, because the clouds are drawing in and we reckon we are in for a rainstorm.

DIARY ENTRY by Karen

We haven't really done anything today except rest and we've booked our flights home and a coach. We leave the Camino on Tuesday, the 11th of June.

Karen sat on the Sarria sign

A welcome rest in a donativo.

OUR CAMINO DIARY - DAY 35
4TH JUNE

Sarria to Portomarin (22.8km)

DIARY ENTRY by Karen

Today has been a mixed day. Although Brett's foot is still painful and suspected tendinitis, he was well rested and did well today. The guidebook made it look like there were a lot of stops, but the reality was that the first stop was after 10km. It rained after an hour and it had been a wet gear day. We stopped for breakfast at Brea, which is at the '102k left' post. The weather broke for a few minutes for us to get a photo at the 100km left marker (which means we have walked 690km+).

We had a choice to make as we came into Portomarin, either the road or the Camino route, it was a challenge as a sheer rock face and the picture does not do it justice and Brett managed extremely well with his poorly limbs.

We walked past a gorgeous harbour lake over the bridge and up more stairs, then arrived at our albergue, washed clothes and crashed. Yesterday we booked our flight home for Tuesday 11th June, so we are now on a time restraint. Today 22.8km.

Diary entry by Brett

We left the comfort of the double bed in the hostel and said goodbye to our host Daniel and went into the darkness of the woods. The material we were walking on in the countryside changed constantly, and we are used to it by now.

Something we haven't seen for a while was a small stone footbridge and today didn't disappoint. We got back on the dusty path, and travelled once again, into the now-familiar wooded areas, through more farmyard towns. The rain arrived, and with it, some cooler, better walking weather.

More footpaths with streams next to them, fed by the rain and an arrow on the side of a building made of cockleshells and painted in yellow. We hit the 100km marker and, as expected, we had our picture taken with the special milestone. Moments later, we started our walk again, this time surrounded by pilgrims. They were everywhere!!!

This 100 km marks the official start of the shortest part of the Camino which anyone can walk to officially gain a Compostela (certificate of completion), and our Pilgrims passports now require two stamps per day. After a couple more kilometres we stopped for tea and Santiago cake, total price €10. We carried on walking and soon noticed a rapid increase in pilgrims' souvenir shops, selling lots of stuff we would have to carry, so decided to wait to buy souvenirs until we got to Santiago. We carried on walking in the rain.

In an effort to take a shortcut, we went down a really rocky route, almost sheer rock face, where I threw my poles down and used the rock walls on either side to clamber down. It lasted almost 1 km. Tarmac road to let us into

Portomarin, with a picture-postcard town and lake with a long bridge, which took us up to approximately 50 to 70 steps, then more walking uphill to our albergue.

These albergues aren't too bad except we can never get the Wi-Fi to work, and the unisex showers had no doors on them. We had pizza for tea and went to bed without a shower.

THOUGHT of the day by Karen.

How easy is it for us to judge? I've had to tell myself off today. The Camino gets busy from this point, as many people walk the last 100 for the certificate. This morning there were the regulars and then a lot of sparkly new people. A lot of the new sparkly people are uni students from around the world who are doing the Camino for credit or as a project, etc... They are walking with lecturers or on their own. The reason for telling myself off is that the peace of the Camino has changed, more people, but also music has been introduced. The students are singing or listening to music; some this morning even had energy to dance with backpacks.

How quick are we to judge others and their motives? Do we alter to the new circumstances or keep talking about the past? Are we willing to move forward into the new and see what other blessings it brings?

We are in an albergue with at least two different groups of students and it's great; the albergue is full of life .

Karen and Brett at the 100km marker

Bridge and lake into Portomarin

We walked down these rocks for about 1km. The picture doesn't do this justice, it took us hours because the rocks had very deep steps, and we had to drop down onto some of them, holding the walls either side to make sure we didn't fall.

OUR CAMINO DIARY - DAY 36
5TH JUNE

Portomarin to Palas de Rei (24km),

Diary entry by Karen

Today has been another challenging day. Within the first 7km it rained, so we had to put on wet weather stuff. We had breakfast at a lovely albergue and because it was still raining and cold, Brett had egg and chips and I had toast. We sat near some ladies from the UK who we have come across a couple of times. As they were leaving, one lady, who was quite taken by Brett and his determination, gave us both a bead angel to accompany us on our journey.

Pressing on, we had sand, mud and clay to deal with, and the weather kept changing, the rain stopped, the sun shone; we dried out and then it rained again and we got drenched again twice more. It was a good excuse for quite a few coffee stops; the second in Ventos, where a lovely blind man was in a church chanting, giving people stamps on their credentials and a blessing. The next one was a donativo albergue which gave free hugs, tea, coffee and snacks run by the Christian organisation, Agape. Brett wanted to do the whole stage today of 24.5km, so pressed on to Palais de Rei. We now have two short days of 15km each. Brett is determined to finish, even with his bad limbs. Hopefully, we will in four days.

Diary entry by Brett

Today was wet from the start. As we walked out of Portomarin with a lot of other pilgrims, we passed lots of buildings. The road constantly changed and always up-and-down. It made today a real slog. We passed chopped down forests, lots of pilgrims, and all the time, the rain was relentless. Toilet stops and food/drink stops were not as frequent, and it made the 24km really tough, especially with my ankle pain.

We stopped at Ligonde and the fuente del peregrinos (the pilgrims fountain), where we found volunteers giving the message of God to weary travellers. Perhaps we may be among the volunteers one day. Later, we found a small church where a blind man was taking donations for blessings and his card, which I stuck inside my diary. We also learnt about the five symbols from the Camino, the yellow arrow, the backpack, bandage, walking stick, and scallop shell.

We arrived at approximately 4:30 pm at Palas de Rei, frozen, and exhausted. I collapsed onto the bed (with signs of hypothermia), and Karen walked 1 km to town to get supplies, then came back to warm up on the bed with a hug for an hour. After that, we had spaghetti Bolognese in the kitchen then went to bed.

. . .

Our Camino Diary - Day 36

THOUGHT of the day by Karen

Albergue San Marcos

We keep chatting every now and again about the simplicity of the Camino and that we are carrying all our possessions. We think it will change things when we are home; what we decide to pack or recycle may be different from before this journey.

We came across a donativo albergue today in Ligonde who are extremely Christian and don't mind telling pilgrims. As you enter, you get a stamp, postcard, offered refreshments and a hug. It was an amazing place to be. It's run by a group of volunteers, all part of the agape organisation.

The track has 5 symbols of the Camino; this is what it says for a backpack

When we were at home, it didn't seem to matter what we put in our backpack. Now that we have to carry it, we realise how much everything weighs and how much each thing counts (Don't forget the count everything guy on Youtube). We also realise how many things we can truly do without. On the Camino of life we all carry a backpack. Sometimes we add things, then we have to carry it, and finally reach the point that it is too much to carry.

What can you take out of your backpack today to make your trip lighter? What excessive baggage are you carrying in life?"

Some interesting questions; we have been getting rid of things along the route and therefore have nothing left to get rid of. But stuff at home is a different matter. We will reflect and think about it.

How about you? What excessive baggage are you carrying in your life?

Inside the donativo prayer corner

Outside the donativo

The sign on the wall outside. Translated, it says,' I am the way and the truth and the life (John 14.6)

OUR CAMINO DIARY - DAY 37
6TH JUNE

Palas de Rei to Melide (14km).

DIARY ENTRY by Karen

We started off in wet weather gear this morning and have stayed in it all day. The walk has been pleasant. We stopped for breakfast and then in Casa Nova for a break and to collect a special wax stamp. The man was a paraplegic and was collecting money for the Olympics.

I picked up a pendant today at a special stamp stand. It says in English "more to a Camino/ path ". On the other side, it has hands, one large and one small. These could represent God holding our hands walking with us or the people we walk with who help us, listen to us and are companions on the journey.

We stopped on the outskirts of Melide and then had a slow walk in.

Look at thought of the day for more about "more to a Camino/path"

. . .

Our Camino Diary - Day 37

DIARY ENTRY by **Brett**

Today was much like any other day to start off with. We headed out into the darkness, down cobble streets with some derelict / half built buildings, past a church and some statues, and straight into a bar/cafe for some breakfast. After that, we passed some more pilgrim souvenir shops, then down through town past some large groups of pilgrims. Moments later, we were walking down flagstone pathways and out into the countryside. Compared to the last few days, the kilometres seemed to fly by and after a few more pilgrim statues pointing us the way, we soon found ourselves at another bar.

This bar, the Casanova, offered something more than just the tea and Santiago cake we were eating... in fact, Karen found it so fantastic and exciting, that she kept stopping people walking past and pointed out to them what was so special. The queue grew and grew, but it was worth it. In order to get the certificate to prove that you have done the Camino de Santiago, you are required to add a rubber ink stamp from the bars and hostels on the way, not all of them, just one or two a day. This bar had a very special stamp... a sello lacre (wax stamp). We stopped, drank our tea, and as Karen invited people in, the queue grew longer. Eventually, I joined the queue, with the understanding that, if you give a donation, you can get a special necklace. I didn't really fancy the necklace (although the one Karen has looked great), but was happy to give a donation for another reason.

I was really hoping I might get a wax stamp for my journal and the credential. When I got to the front of the queue, I bravely struck up a conversation and showed the man my journal with all of its scraps of information inside. I asked him, and to my surprise, with a great big queue behind me, he not only gave me a wax stamp for my credential and journal, but even embossed one of the pages, and stamped the outside of my journal with a special large stamp. I was so surprised and thanked him very much, popping a donation in the box.

We carried on walking, arrived in Melide at approx 1pm and got into our albergue, falling asleep for about 3 hours before heading out to have tea.

When we came back, we met our roommates, had a coffee and went to bed.

Today was a much easier day at only 15km, tomorrow is also 15km to Arzua.

Thought of the day by Karen

One thing we have realised here is the real Camino begins or continues when we get home. All of life is reflected here with its joys and sorrows, it's a time of happiness and laughter and times of suffering.

On the track from yesterday is a story inspired by the encounter between Jesus and the rich young man.

One day a young pilgrim arrived at the monastery searching for an elderly pilgrim who was known to the wisest of them all. Despite his youth, he had already completed one of the most well-known pilgrimages of the world.

He approached the wise man and asked, "Master, what must I do to become a true pilgrim?" The elderly man looked into his eyes and felt great compassion for him.

"Son, if you truly wish to be an authentic pilgrim, return to your home with your family, your neighbours and your friends and listen to them, serve them, forgive them and love them. Then you will be a true pilgrim."

The young man laid down his walking stick, turned

around and left deeply saddened. He was willing to walk thousands of kilometres, even carrying a tremendous amount of weight on his shoulders, but he was unwilling to fulfill what the wise man advised him to do.

We are all pilgrims in life. Some of us are people of faith, and some are not. Yet each of us can choose to take up the challenge of the authentic pilgrim; to listen, serve, forgive and love those people around us that God has placed on our journey.

Lord, may we each be true authentic pilgrims, choosing to give selflessly, to listen, serve, forgive and love all around us. Amen

This translates to "More to a Camino/path"

This is the usual wax stamp for the credential (complete with ribbon and camino shell).

My special wax stamp on the outside of my journal. La Huella del Peregrino translates to "The pilgrims footsteps".

OUR CAMINO DIARY - DAY 38
7TH JUNE

Melide to Arzua (15km)

Diary entry by Brett

Erm... not sure what to say. Not much happened today, we got up rather late (7:30am), walked through some woods which were filled with eucalyptus trees, and then got to our hostel (with pretty much no pain, although we did only walk 15k, oh, and Karen lost her kindle :((If you ever want to do the Camino, don't bring a kindle, that's both of ours gone in a month, but hey, kindles can be replaced, experiences like the Camino can not).

However.... this evening was amazing. Instead of the usual pilgrim meal of salad, paella, steak and chips, etc... we went for pizza.

We walked up and down the high street of Arzúa for about 45 minutes, then back to our albergue and found a place within minutes of our albergue.

. . .

DIARY ENTRY by Karen

Today was an uneventful day and nothing really to report. It was a pleasant walk, through parks and pathways. We walked through parts of eucalyptus trees (which was unique to see the bark peeling off at the root). Even though we left later this morning, we still arrived at the albergue by 1 pm.

We ended up at a hostel called "The Way" which is quite apt. It was a bit more expensive, but the facilities were great. We went out for tea to the best pizza restaurant in Spain. It was massive and tasted so good.

THOUGHT of the day by Karen

While we have been here, as well as reading novels, I am reading 'how to pray' by Pete Greig. It is an amazing book, and the best prayer book I have ever read. Pete's book is a practical 'this is how to do it' book, no fluff, really honest and down-to-earth analogies. The foreword is by Nicki Gumbel and the Methodist church are endorsing it.

One topic is intercessory prayer. We have felt people praying for us. Especially in the last few days.

Brett has been walking better and even wanting to go for a wander the last couple of nights and enjoying the walk during the day. We can vouch that prayer works.

How is your prayer life? Are you as close to God as you want to be? (Check out the book).

Lord, thank you for those people that pray for us and intercede on our behalf. Bless them, we pray. Amen

Fabio cooking our pizza.

Our mahoooosive pizza reached all the way across the table !!!

The clock with no hands simply says "There is no time here today, enjoy your Camino".

OUR CAMINO DIARY - DAY 39
8TH JUNE

Arzua to O' Pedrouzo (20km)

DIARY ENTRY by Brett

After setting off much earlier this morning, we walked through the streets of Arzua into the misty paths and through the woods. We met a beautiful white horse, clearly someone's pride and joy, as it was well looked after, with a trimmed mane, well-clipped coat, and lovely flowing tail.

We carried on through the woods, almost surrounded by the thick fog. After a quick stop to collect a passport stamp, we walked past a man crafting beautiful Camino walking sticks. Later, we found ourselves on the road crossing a bridge, and looking down we saw a wide motorway with the usual 2 to 3 cars of Spain's rush hour traffic along its entire length.

As we stepped off the bridge, we were completely overwhelmed with pilgrims, way more than in the last few days. We all walked through more eucalyptus forests and met a couple of American priests on sabbatical.

More muddy track and trees later, we found a bar with beer bottle trees. The bar owners had sold the beers to happy pilgrims, and each bottle then became a part of the beer tree arboretum, with comments in white pen from pilgrims on every single bottle.

More muddy tracks later, and we stopped for some ginger lemonade. The waiter even gave me the recipe. It was amazing.

More walking, and it was time for another stop, this time... lunch. We ate outside as usual, and a man's behaviour caught Karen's attention. He seemed to be selling something, but no-one was interested.

We finished our food and headed off down the road.

The arrows took us past the man, and as we drew closer, we noticed some signs... curious. We looked further and saw some inspirational quotes. Further along was a table with a stamp, and some books. The man told us that the book was his story of the Camino he had taken with his dog in 2007. I jumped at the chance to have a stamp in my journal. Karen donated some money for the book, and he personalised it for us, then looked at my journal, and personalised that too, then gave us each a hug. Moments later, as I was packing my journal back in my bag, he was inundated with people who wanted to buy his book.

We left, and headed towards our hostel, grabbed our beds, then rested.

Later, we went to mass at the church, and had tea afterwards.

Tomorrow.... Santiago!!!

Diary entry by Karen

Today was a wonderful walk. Brett was walking better. It

started off cold and windy and when we got to the breakfast stop. It was all outside, so we continued on to the next place. The coldness went after a few hours, and it was a pleasant walk, mainly through eucalyptus trees.

The major highlight of the day was in Santa Iruña when we came across a lovely space that had been created. Extremely sacred and spiritual. There was a man giving out sweets and stamps. We noticed a book that had the most beautiful cover. It was his story of doing the Camino in 2007 with his dog. I decided to buy one. He has personally written in the cover, signed and dated it. I'm looking forward to reading it once we are home. We made it into the village at 2pm, we found our albergue at the end of town and rested.

Beautiful white horse

Selfie time with the author of the book "shared solitude", all about his journey on the Camino with him and his dog.

The massive shell inside the church

OUR CAMINO DIARY - DAY 40
9TH JUNE - PENTECOST SUNDAY.

O' Pedrouzo to Santiago.

Diary entry by Brett

We left in darkness again, soon swamped by more pilgrims, and came across a tent with another pilgrim in it. He was asleep, but his t-shirt and banner said that he was travelling the Camino with no money and gave a Facebook page to read more. On the floor was some food, a bowl with some change in it, and a couple of other things. We donated a bag of supermarket shopping for him and left him to sleep.

A couple of kilometres later, we hit the 15k mark.... Only 15km left !!! And stopped at the bar appropriately named kilometro 15 for a drink of Kas Limon, tea, and some breakfast.

Walking further on, we saw the guy we bumped into yesterday who invited us to mass. We walked in and got another pilgrim passport stamp.

More wood walking later, and we stopped for another drink (its thirsty work, this walking thing).

Coming out of the bar and up the street (lots of stairs, pffft) we came across a man who had a donation with wire-frame pilgrims (flat wire art made of crafting wire) and stopped for another stamp. This time, I stamped my journal as I was running out of space on my pilgrims' passport. His stamp was hand carved from a rubber (eraser).

We walked further up the road and spoke to a lady vicar from the UK, also on sabbatical, and after chatting to her for a bit, we bumped into the Australian ladies from last night. Mother and daughter were celebrating the daughter's birthday today, so what a day!!!

Further on, we stopped at the Mount of Joy... in this unique place, if you stand in the right place and look in the right direction, you can see the towers of Santiago cathedral. So... we stood, we looked, and we saw it. We both took photos, and none of them turned out well. Lol.

We grabbed another Kas Limon (seriously, this stuff is amazing, why don't we have it in the UK?) and an ice cream and carried on.

After the pain of the last few weeks with my ankle and knee, I set myself a challenge. After using my walking sticks as crutches for the last two weeks..... I was determined to walk the last 15k without them... so; I packed them away, and we walked slowly to Santiago.

The last few weeks have been fantastic for measuring where we are, based on the way markers with their accurate count, but as we neared Santiago, they just seemed to disappear... the waymarkers were there, but the count wasn't :(

Eventually, we got to Santiago, slightly lost, and wondering where on earth the cathedral was, we finally found it. Woohoo! After a quick selfie, we bumped into

Gracie from the US, and her mum Cori (I had nicknamed Gracie 'Miss Coolsocks' because she had some really funky socks!), we took some photos with them, and then bumped into some Spanish pilgrims we had spoken to, and had photos with them also. Then we went to find a place to stay for the night.

The monastery we found is huuuuuuuge, in fact, it's that big, we had to climb the stairs to get to the lift, lol.

It has showers with doors - yay :)

It has its own supermarket on the bottom floor, an amazing rest area, leather chairs. Seriously, you could mistake this place for a hotel.

A quick shower, and we headed off into the city, and one of our Camino friends (Susan from America) wanted to meet up with us. We had to go and get our Compostela (certificate of completion) and it took forever to queue for it. Eventually, we both had two certificates in Latin and Spanish with our names on, one for completion, and one for the distance award.

After lots of confusion, lousy phone signal, waiting around and faffing about, we were tired, hungry and also missed out on the opportunity to meet up with our Camino friend, but we had our Compostelas. Hopefully she is around tomorrow. Until then, we have gone back (after tea) to the Albergue, to get some much-needed rest.

My challenge? I completed it... I walked the last 15k into Santiago without walking poles, and the last 2k we walked into the city holding hands together.... we had done it!

One more post to go.... check it out tomorrow.

DIARY ENTRY by Karen

We left quite early while others were sleeping. We

walked 5km through roads to our breakfast stop. It was a busy place but well worth waiting. We had warmed croissants and a hot drink. They had a fantastic poster of the Camino that I would like to have. Brett decided at this point he wanted to walk the last 15 km without his sticks. With all of his injuries, he's been using his sticks as crutches.

We noticed over the next stretch strange things there was a man sat on a log, obviously out of breath. He said he was okay, but about 20 minutes later, he was in front of us on another log. It seems strange, and I had the sense that he was an angel. It made me realise that as well as it being our last day, it was also a spiritual battle going on.

If Brett completed, it would be the first thing he had been allowed to complete in his life. He will be different after this experience. Whatever was hanging over his head has been broken. We had some climbing to do up to the Mount of Joy and had our first view of the cathedral. We had a rest of Kas Limon and ice cream before tackling the last 5 km. The walk into town was mostly on the road. We came across an ornate sign for the Santiago Compostela, and took a selfie.

We walked to the cathedral with backpacks on and walked past all the albergues. On the way into the cathedral square I felt quite emotional, as I do now, writing this. To think we completed such an adventure is hard to comprehend. But we made it through everything that we have experienced and gone through. We are staying at a monastery which is amazing. We have collected our Compostelas and certificate of distance.

On the year we did the Camino, the outside of the Cathedral had just had all of it's scaffolding removed, after years of external restoration, and work had started on the inside. This meant that we were not able to see the sight of the Botefumeiro, a large swinging incense burner, swung from one end of the Cathedral to the other, to get ride of the smell of the Pilgrims, once they had finished their journey, or to take part in the Pilgrims Mass, but we did still get the chance to visit the resting place of St.James.

THOUGHT of the day by Karen.

We have walked 20km today into Santiago. As we were coming in, it reminded me of all the people we have met over the past 40 days. We have said hello and goodbye to so many people. Some we know made it to Santiago and others we can only hope they did. It was strange walking into the Cathedral Square and them not being there. It was quite an emotional moment walking in and having that sense that we had made it.

All of today has had me thinking about when we die and what happens. I think it will be like today but 100% better. As a Christian, I believe that there is life after death. I believe that when we die and go to what we call heaven, all the people who have been important in our lives and have died before us will be there cheering us on. There will be no doubts or hoping people have made it. You will see them, we will know. There is a party in heaven for every person who becomes a believer. I bet there is a party in heaven for every believer that is called home too.

The statue on the Mount of Joy

Selfie walking into Santiago

Our Camino Diary - Day 40

0 km at our hostel

Brett outside Cathedral, there were literally hundreds of cyclists outside, in groups that had just finished the Camino.

The cathedral selfie at Santiago de Compostela.

SABBATICAL REPORT

At the end of the Camino, and as a part of her sabbatical, Karen was expected to write a report. This is the report of her experiences, and what it meant to her on her christian walk with God.

Sabbatical report

<u>Camino</u>

This report is not long enough to express all that happened during the Camino journey. Below is a fragrance and some insights. These insights are based on 'Beatitudes of the Pilgrim', created by a nun from Pamplona who has walked the Camino.

We left St Jean Pied-de-Port on 1st May and arrived in Santiago on 9th July 2019 (Pentecost Sunday). We had walked over 540+ miles (769 km) during those forty days.

→

<u>Beatitudes of the Pilgrim</u>

Blessed are you pilgrim, if you discover the Camino opens your eyes to what is not seen.

While away, we had some bad ascents and descents, and we did loads of things before tackling them, but they weren't as bad as we had made them out to be; and not worth the worry and stress. I have learnt instead of procrastinating, to take heart and just do it, the relief afterwards is great. Mark Forster encourages breaking things down to the least resistance and then action it.

Blessed are you pilgrim, if what concerns you most is not to arrive, as to arrive with others.

I learnt very quickly that we all walk at different paces. Many people would shoot off and you wouldn't see them for a few hours, or until the next hostel. We had to learn as a couple to walk together. It was apparent at the start that I would go racing off and often left Brett behind. It took us nearly two weeks to walk the same pace (me going slower and Brett walking a little quicker). This is a major step in our marriage and a lesson we are taking into life with us.

Blessed are you, pilgrim, when you contemplate the Camino and you discover it is full of names and dawns.

We met so many amazing people from all around the world who shared such personal things about themselves quickly. It has helped me to be more assertive in introducing myself to others and showing an interest in their life. It was and always is, a privilege to listen to the stories of others. You learn to lean on each other for support, encouragement, and advice.

Blessed are you pilgrim, if your knapsack is empty of things and your heart does not know where to hang so many feelings and emotions.

Little blessings are so important, i.e. Someone offering you water, a plaster, some medication. I also became aware of how important God's garden was to me. We saw some amazing views from mountain-tops to valley-deep and all part of God's world. It was truly stunning.

Blessed are you pilgrim, if you discover that one step back to help another is more valuable than a hundred forward without seeing what is at your side.

→

During the last two weeks of our pilgrimage, Brett was injured. This meant that he was slower than before and needed more breaks. It was an excellent opportunity to be mindful of everything else around us. It also meant that we noticed when others were struggling and could offer them help. Several times, Brett suggested I walk faster to get to a destination quicker, but I stayed with him and we stayed with others because we discovered it was more valuable to take a step back to help another.

Blessed are you pilgrim, when you don't have words to give thanks for everything that surprises you at every twist and turn of the way.

This pilgrimage has made me think about possessions and the luxuries of life. I think this experience has made me more thankful and a little less consumerist. I think it will make us think about what we class as 'essentials'. During packing for our coming move, we have donated to charity and decluttered more than we would've done before this experience.

Blessed are you pilgrim, if you search for the truth and make of the Camino a life, and of your life a way, in search of the one who is the way, the truth and the life.

I have learnt so much as part of this Sabbatical Pilgrimage that will become part of my life; one example is... wanting to stay fit. We struggled at the start of the Camino because we were not fit. This experience has encouraged me to stay fit now. Therefore, I have taken up running since returning home. I am using an app called 'couch to 5k'. Once I have finished this challenge, I intend to do the park run in my new location weekly as a way of keeping myself fit, and getting to know the community and mission.

Blessed are you pilgrim, if on the way you meet yourself and gift yourself with time without rushing so as not to disregard the image in your heart.

I am the type of person who needs to be busy all the time. The problem with walking 18-32km each day is that you need to rest and take 'siestas'. It was a real blessing to find (on the Camino) time to be me, time to let the dross of life drop off, time to read and relax, time to spend with others. I learnt a lot about myself in the silence of each day. I intend to put into place a good working pattern so that I can continue to have a 'siesta' kind of experience within ministry.

Blessed are you pilgrim if you discover the Camino holds a lot of silence and the silence prayer and the prayer of meeting with God, who is waiting for you.

I realised on this pilgrimage that I had become so busy leading others into the presence of God; I had neglected my spirituality. This journey has renewed my faith, spirituality, and the importance of looking after myself within the constraints of ministry. It has also made me realise that changing the location doesn't change the habits. Decide to change habits and form new ones. I am going to make sure in my next appointment that I put as much priority on 'being', as well as 'doing'; therefore, keeping myself spiritually nourished.

It has given me some ideas and techniques to take into my own church councils and circuit meetings this coming year, while discussing this business.

Another learning was being a world buddy. We had Rev Castro allocated to our district. Rev Castro spoke no English and therefore communicating was interesting. I was pleased that I had learnt a little Spanish before the Camino. I could sort of communicate with him with the aid of signs. Even though I took up Spanish to help on the Camino, I intend to keep learning the language. I think it will be a superb skill in the years to come.

→

<u>Tools for ministry</u>

Lastly, I wanted to make sure that I was properly resourced for taking on my new stationing, especially because I am going as superintendent for the first time. I have read the following two books that I have gleaned some excellent advice and techniques from.

Reading Mark Forster 'Get everything done and still have time to play,' and Brené Brown 'Dare to Lead,'

I have also read two bullet journaling guides after coming across this technique on YouTube three years ago. Since then, I have been trying it out and have found it to be the best way to order my ministry. I wanted to read the guides to fine-tune the system I have been using to become an excellent system that enables and supports ministry. I am now confident that I am moving into my new role, as well prepared as I can be.

OUR CAMINO DIARY - MORE PICTURES.

10 Jun 2019
Santiago de Compostela

Last post by Brett
A massive Thankyou.

Before you read the final section, Karen and I would like to say that although this book has been about ourselves and our Camino, and even though you weren't here with us, we are amazed at how many lovely comments, posts, texts, emails and other things people sent us, to keep us going, and we would like to thank you for buying this book.

It certainly has been a trip of a lifetime and one that has taught us many things. Going back to basics helped us to get in touch with who we really are. It's definitely strengthened our relationship as a couple and also with God.

We couldn't have done it without all the different experiences and support along the way, and as most of these haven't been written about, we have come up with a few things that we have loved and some things which are best left on the Camino (it's good to share).

Today we finished our Camino by visiting the remains of St. James, the apostle in his silver casket (the very reason for this pilgrimage). It was a very surreal experience. Tomorrow, we fly home, and then the real Camino (way / journey) starts.

Post by Karen
  Santiago de Compostela
  We thought that our Camino ended yesterday, but how wrong we were. We went this morning to the English pilgrims mass at the pilgrims office.

  It was a beautiful service and afterwards they invited us into the English office for a cuppa and chat. Afterwards, as we were trying to come down the stairs, a man stopped Brett and invited him in for a free massage. He is a qualified Physiotherapist; he has worked on his leg, ankle and knee, which is now almost back to being right, but still sore, and gave him some advice for his ankle (lots of rest and frozen peas). While I was waiting, I watched an amazing reflection in the pilgrims chapel to help you think deeper about your Camino journey. It included a great Beatitude for Pilgrims

  Then this afternoon we have been to the Cathedral museum and the Cathedral. We have walked past St. James and into the crypt where his remains are.

  We have had such a spirit filled day, that was not planned at all.

  Thank you Lord

Our Camino Diary - More Pictures.

Another selfie from the top of the cathedral balcony

Some of our Camino friends from the United States of America (Miss Cool Socks and her Mum).

Some of our Camino friends from Spain.

Pilgrims in the square from top of Cathedral balcony

St James himself.

FUNNY THINGS WE MISS...
... AND SOME THINGS WE DON'T.

The following is a list of things we found funny, interesting or confusing differences between home life and the Camino.

These lists are the ones that stick out the most and are not intended to sway your decision, and if you decide to do the Camino yourself, we wish you Buen Camino (Good way)

Things we miss from home

- family and friends
- Home-cooked meals
- Sausages (they don't even do pepperoni on pizzas, we had chorizo instead (I recommend it))
- Vegetables
- Mash,
- Jeans

Things we will miss from the Camino

- the sense of friendship and camaraderie.
- The peace and quiet
- The sights, sounds and smells of everything natural.
- The stars

- The sunrises and sunsets
- That Christmas feeling every day, because people are so nice to each other.
- Ice cream after every evening meal
- KAS LIMON (This stuff is the staple drink on the Camino - someone call the company and tell them to sell it in the UK, please)
- Cupboards above the sink, with no cupboard bottom and draining racks instead of shelves, so instead of wiping up, simply wash up, put the plates away and they drip dry inside the cupboard, into the sink. Amazing and so innovative!
- The rush hour traffic of three cars now and then on the motorways
- Watching Netflix on the bottom bunk with my phone jammed in the slats of the top bunk so I can just lie down and look upwards to watch the film.
- Watching Netflix on the top bunk using my selfie stick jammed into my bum bag so I can look upwards and lie down
- Napolitanas and massive croissants
- Being able to eat late and never getting heart burn
- No artificial additives, colourings, or sweeteners.
- Everyone saying Buen Camino

Things we won't miss, lol

- chucking used toilet roll into a bin to be recycled instead of down the toilet... (so that's how their water is so clean!!).
- random items from Karen's top bunk falling off from under her pillow and through the gaps onto me, lol
- Bee stings and bug bites (although I can now look back at it and laugh).

- Sleeping with all of our valuables inside the bottom of the sleeping bag, (to prevent them ending up lost or stolen) lol
- fumbling around in the shower in complete darkness for the light switch when the timer finishes after 4 minutes and the water is still going lol
- Cold showers (brrrr).
- Unisex showers with no doors. Come on... seriously?
- Waving your arms around like a wally trying to get the movement activated lights to switch on in the toilets or showers after being plunged into complete darkness
- Wearing shoes in the shower to prevent our feet from getting covered in many nasties, including athletes' foots, verrucas, etc
- Wiping your knife and fork after using them for the first course and saving them to use in the second course (Brett never got used to this)
- People farting
- People snoring
- People who complain about others snoring... and then snoring themselves, lol
- Banging my head on the bottom bunk
- Fear of falling out of the top bunk
- Fear of the bunk falling apart (some of these things are literally held together with tie wraps, I kid you not)
- People rustling loud plastic bags at 5am in the morning.
- That person who switches on the dorm light at 5:30am waking everyone up at once
- No toilet roll (make sure you pack one).
- Automatic dorm lights
- Wi-Fi that allows you to sign up for a code to be sent to

your phone, but the text never arrives, so no Wi-Fi lol (always happened in the municipals).

- Having to shave using the lemon lush bar and a shaving brush. Lol.

- Paper bedsheets (we know they are there for hygiene, but they are slippery, crinkly, noisy and uncomfortable)

- Mattresses with that "a million people slept in this bed" dip, which you can't actually turn over because you just fall back into the dip, lol

- People who complain they are cold, close the window next to you and then leave the window across the dorm open all night, lol

ABOUT THE AUTHOR

Brett Jackson lives in Merseyside, UK, with his wife Karen. When not spending time with their children, he spends his time as a new author writing sci-fi books, watching films, reading, and walking. Brett would like one day to be able to create a name for himself, and prove to all of his teachers at school, that he could make it as a writer. Until then, he is happy with daydreaming and getting paid for it.

facebook.com/brettishbooks

PLEASE LEAVE A REVIEW.
… AND SHOW YOUR SUPPORT.

We hope you enjoyed *Our Camino Diary*.

Please show your support by leaving a review, so that other people can enjoy this book. Just a few words would help other readers to know whether this book is the right one for them, and help me as an independent author.

Thankyou.

ONE LAST THING.

Please sign up to the newsletter at https://www.brettishbooks.com to receive updates about the books I write.

It's completely free and I won't send you spam, that's a promise :)

Printed in Great Britain
by Amazon